LIFE W[...]
COSMOS'
CLEARANCE

DANIEL M. SALTER

as told to *Nancy Red Star*

A gent Daniel M. Salter is a retired former counterintelligence agent for the *Scientific and Technical Unit of Interplanetary Phenomena* in Washington D.C.. He was a member of the Pilot Air Force, NRO (National Reconnaissance Office) and DCCCD (Development of Conscious Contact Citizenry Department) with the United States military. He was a CON-RAD courier for President Eisenhower, with a clearance far above Top Secret (Cosmos) and a member of the original *Project Blue Book*. His expertise was in radar and electronics, his field of investigation UFOs, Aliens and Particlization. Now seventy-five, Salter has both Comanche and French ancestry.

Fig. i. "EBE" by Christopher Schott.

LIFE WITH A
COSMOS
CLEARANCE

DANIEL M. SALTER
as told to Nancy Red Star

LIGHT Technology PUBLISHING

ISBN 1-891824-37-6

Published by

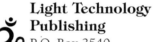

**Light Technology
Publishing**
P.O. Box 3540
Flagstaff, AZ 86003
1-800-450-0985
e-mail: publishing@lighttechnology.com
www.lighttechnology.com

Agent Daniel M. Salter is a retired former counterintelligence agent for the Interplanetary Phenomenon Scientific and Technical Unit in Washington, D.C. He was a pilot in the Air Force, National Reconnaissance Office (NRO) operative and a member of the Development of Conscious Contact Citizenry Department (DCCCD) with the United States military. He was a Conrad courier for President Eisenhower, with a clearance far above Top Secret (Cosmos), and a member of the original Project Blue Book. His expertise was in radar and electronics; his field of investigation UFOs, aliens and particlization. Now seventy-five, Salter has reclaimed his Comanche ancestry.

*This book is dedicated to the harmonics of light technology
and the temple pyramid at Tula, Mexico.*

ACKNOWLEDGMENTS

Thanks to:

My beloved mother, Joyce Burroughs Matthews, and my
great-grandfathers, Joseph Matthews and John Burroughs;

Agent Daniel M.Salter and family,
all the participants of the Disclosure Project and
Dr. Steven M.Greer;

O'Ryin Swanson and Light Technology Publishing;

Editors: the late Margaret Pinyan, Laura Monroe, Birgit Buss
and the editorial staff at Light Technology Publishing;

Southside Copy, Copy Queen, Richard's Photo Lab,
Channel Two Public Access, Photoworks and my webmaster Lynda Bauline
and Elizabeth Gallegos;

All of the artists who contributed their work.

Christopher Schott
(208) 660-0613

Jingalu
www.dreamtimegallery.com

Scott Preston Collins
(817) 244-3865

Darline Destephen
Darline2005@aol.com

NANCY RED STAR

CONTENTS

You have been telling the people that this is the Eleventh Hour.
Now you must go back and tell people that this is the Hour.
And there are things to be considered:
Where are you living?
What are you doing?
What are your relationships?
Are you in the right relation?
Where is your water?
Know your garden.
It is time to speak your truth.
Create your community.
Be good to each other.
And do not look outside yourself for the leader.
This could be a good time!
There is a river flowing now very fast.
It is so great and swift that there are those who will be afraid.
They will try to hold on to the shore.
They will feel they are being torn apart, and they will suffer greatly.
Know the river has its destination.
The elders say we must let go of the shore,
push off into the river,
keep our eyes open,
and our heads above the water.
See who is in there with you and celebrate.
At this time in history, we are to take nothing personally.
Least of all ourselves.
For the moment that we do, our spiritual growth
and journey comes to a halt.
The time of the lone wolf is over. Gather yourselves!
Banish the word struggle from your attitude and your vocabulary.
All that we do now must be done in a sacred manner and in celebration.
We are the ones we've been waiting for.

—THE ELDERS
Oraibi, Arizona
Hopi Nation

The Washington Times

Government is covering up UFO evidence, group says

The U.S. government has been covering up evidence of extraterrestrial visits for more than 50 years, an array of 20 retired Air Force, Federal Aviation Administration and intelligence officers said yesterday.

They demanded Congress hold hearings on what they say is longstanding secret U.S. involvement with UFOs and extraterrestrials.

Calling it the "greatest secret of the 20th century," the officials, who termed themselves "witnesses" of UFO-related events, described a series of military investigations they said they saw: crashes of alien spacecraft, bodies of alien beings, secret government documents, even James Bond-style "erasures" of people who knew too much.

"The individuals who have these sightings range from airline pilots and military pilots to police officers, some of the people your lives depend on, on a daily basis," retired Air Force Lt. Col. Charles Brown told a roomful of skeptical reporters.

"They are very reputable, dependable people," he said.

"The field is filled with hoaxes and scams," said Dr. Steven Greer, director of the Disclosure Project, which had gathered the witnesses. "But it doesn't mean all of it is."

The 20 witnesses, he said, were a fraction of the 400 people who are willing to testify under oath—and under congressional immunity—about a secretive portion of the government they say has gone out of control.

UFOs have long fascinated Americans, including several U.S. presidents. Webster L. Hubbell, a former associate attorney general under

President Clinton, has described in an autobiography his unsuccessful quest to determine government involvement in the topic.

John Callahan, a former FAA division chief of accidents and investigations, said he was directed by CIA officers to cover up a Nov. 18, 1986, incident involving a UFO and a Japanese airliner near Anchorage, Alaska.

"We were all sworn to secrecy that this event never happened," he said.

Michael Smith, a former U.S. Air Force air traffic controller stationed near Klamath Falls, Ore., in the 1960s and early 1970s, reported seeing a UFO hovering at 80,000 feet one night.

"I was told you keep it to yourself," he said. "NORAD [North American Aerospace Defense Command] called me one night to say there's a UFO coming up the California coastline. I asked them what to do. They said nothing, not to write it down."

After he was stationed at another military base in Michigan, UFOs were so close to one landing strip, he said, that two incoming B-52s had to be steered around them.

The Disclosure Project, a Crozet, Va.-based research organization that has been gathering government witnesses for several years, says its reason for going public is because the U.S. government has long had information on anti-gravity propulsion systems. These have been retrieved from downed spacecraft, such as those from a purported crash in Roswell, N.M., in July 1947.

These propulsion systems, which would use electromagnetic and "zero point energy state" technology to produce vast amounts of energy without any pollution, would drastically change the world's oil-based economy. Such energy sources would not require damming the world's rivers or building power plants, transmission lines or other expensive infrastructures needed to produce electricity for the world's 6 billion inhabitants.

Such electro-gravitic technology would also allow people to travel totally above the ground, rendering roads obsolete. Several witnesses talked of incredible speeds demonstrated by these crafts, estimated by radar technicians to be more than 10,000 miles an hour. The fastest known speed of a man-made aircraft is 3,000 miles an hour.

But information on extraterrestrial speeds is never made public, said Daniel Sheehan, counsel for Project Disclosure. Even the Vatican Library, he said, has hidden information on UFOs.

Donna Hare, a NASA design illustrator with secret clearance, said UFOs were routinely airbrushed out of high altitude photos of the Earth before being released to the public.

"We always airbrush them out before we release them to the public," one technician told her. Curious, she began asking around the agency.

"A guard told me he was asked to burn some photographs and not look at them," she said. "And there was another guard guarding him, watching him burn the photographs. He looked at one and it was a picture of a UFO and he immediately was hit in the head and had a big gash in his forehead."

Apollo astronauts, she said, had spotted UFOs, but they "are told to keep this quiet and not to talk about it," she said. One of them, Edgar Mitchell, who walked on the moon as part of the Apollo 14 team, is a witness for Project Disclosure.

Karl Wolf, an Air Force sergeant who was assigned to the National Security Agency, said that mysterious structures were discovered on the far side of the moon when the United States was mapping its surface before the 1969 lunar landing. Those photos too were culled out of the public record.

The Pentagon does not comment on UFOs, except to say they do not exist and that such objects really are high altitude balloons, swamp gas or military aircraft.

Despite the government's refusal to discuss the issue, several witnesses have also told of being stationed at military bases or near silos containing nuclear missiles when a UFO swung by. Afterward, military officers would discover the missiles had been temporarily deactivated.

CHAPTER ONE

THE DISCLOSURE PROJECT

On May 9, 2001, the Disclosure Project, a nonprofit research and public interest group, hosted a major event at the National Press Club in Washington, D.C. This historic event included witness testimony from twenty to twenty-five military, intelligence, government and corporate individuals who were involved with UFO projects over the past fifty years. Selected witnesses had previously met in closed meetings with members of Congress and staff on Capitol Hill, as well as administration leaders and White House and Pentagon staff and officials. Then, on May 9, the larger group of witnesses presented their information before a worldwide group of media correspondents.

Among the ex-military witnesses were Major General Vasily Alexeyev; USAF Lt. Col. Dwynne Arneson; USAF Lt. Col. Charles Brown; USAF Capt. Robert Salas, SAC launch controller; Merle Shane McDow of the USN Atlantic Command; Major George A. Filer III, USAF Intelligence; Army Sgt. Clifford Stone; Astronaut Dr. Edgar Mitchell; Lt. Col. Joe Wojtecki; USAF Col. Ross Dedrickson; Michael Smith, former USAF air traffic controller; Graham Bethune, former Navy commander pilot with a Top Secret clearance; and myself, Chief Master Sergeant Dan Salter, former USAF and NRO operative with a Cosmos clearance. Some of those who were not in the military included Don Phillips, Lockheed Skunkworks, USAF and CIA contractor; John Callahan, FAA division chief who headed the Accidents and Investigations Office; Dr. Paul Czysz and Dr. Robert Wood, both McDonnell Douglas engineers; Nick Pope, British Ministry of Defense official; Donna Hare, NASA employee; Neil Daniels, United Airlines pilot; and Dr. Carol Rosin, missile defense consultant and former spokesperson for Wernher von Braun. There was a live webcast of this event at 9 A.M., and over 250,000 people were online earlier, waiting for the press conference to begin. (The next webcast event held at the National Press Club drew only about 25,000.) People literally jammed the wires, according to Connect Live, which hosted the webcast for the National Press Club. Thousands of people from all corners of the globe watched the event online. Word is that the National Security Agency (NSA) scrambled and blocked some media outlets.

Those of us who were military witnesses of UFO history showed official government documentation with our detailed testimony. Our focus was and is on the facts and documents. Our purpose was and is to get the mainstream media and government officials to hear those facts and move us toward an honest congressional inquiry.

Fig. 1. Disclosure Project, May 9, 2001. Testimony at the
National Press Club in Washington, D.C.

Since then the Disclosure Project has had dozens of interviews with major media worldwide. These include NBC's *Dateline*, CBS, CNN and BBC radio. News articles have appeared in *Pravda*, the Chinese media, the *Washington Times,* the UK *Sunday Times* and Televisa in Latin America.

The Disclosure Project was initiated in 1993 by Steven Greer, M.D., to identify firsthand military and government witnesses to UFO events and projects who would be used in a public disclosure when it became safe to do so. He interviewed about four hundred such people throughout the world and in every armed service in the U.S. (and many from the UK and Russia), as well as in the National Reconnaissance Office (NRO), NASA, the Defense Intelligence Agency (DIA) and so on. Over a hundred of these interviews have been filmed. Greer knew that the last congressional hearings on UFOs were held in 1968 by the House Committee on Science and Astronautics of the 90th Congress in its second session; it was called the Symposium on Unidentified Flying Objects. There had been no hearings since then, until he was able to speak to closed sessions of various committees after he had gathered much impressive testimony.

A seed has been planted by those who are part of the Disclosure Project by their meetings with members of Congress and the White House offices. It is of the utmost importance, we believe, that each citizen—not only of this country but of the world—participates in this project of disclosure. We who came forward want to ban weapons from space and stop aggressively shooting down space vehicles and their extraterrestrial occupants. We need to declassify the advanced electromagnetic propulsion systems in use by the secret government and start producing them for the world to use, thereby helping to save this planet. As the dark veil of secrecy lifts, the shadow itself is becoming transparent. I believe that the Internet has been seeded by the extraterrestrials to enable this lifting of the veil so the information can be disseminated.

I was initially interviewed for *The Disclosure Project* documentary in December 2000.[1] I was comfortable about going public because of the many other military personnel who were involved. It reassured me to know that so many military people were coming forth and talking. I had never told what I knew to any public or private group, only to friends and family in personal conversations. I'm no longer alone in coming forward publicly.

Fig. 2. Disclosure Project Organizer Steven Greer, M.D., speaking to the
National Press Club.

The people who were employed in agencies within the military and knew the truth about UFOs had been sworn to secrecy. William Cooper became my mentor after I read his book *Behold a Pale Horse* and talked to him.[2] I knew my time would come. Now I am finally relieved to speak the truth. We military men who hold on to this knowledge are getting old and dying, and we want the truth to come out. We will either do it ourselves or leave it for our children and wives to do.

Personally, I have told those on Capitol Hill that I am being led to this by the extraterrestrials themselves. They have convinced me that it is time. They have been waiting on the government, and if the government does not come forward with the truth, then the ETs will take a more public role in disclosure.

As we testify before Congress, representing a military group, we are freed of our secrecy oaths. There is no need to be secret anymore. Who is our enemy? Wernher von Braun warned us that we would be told that first our enemies would be Russia, then terrorism, then the extraterrestrials. We want to drop the veil of secrecy because the public has the right to know. We are losing out on many advanced technologies and new energy sources that can stop the pollution of the Earth. By keeping these secret and continuing to use internal combustion engines, we destroy our environment. We don't have to do this; we could convert to electromagnetic propulsion systems that pollute nothing and use no fuel.

Electromagnetism is a free source of energy, not only throughout our planet but throughout the universe. We are now at a crisis of technology. We have a global ecological emergency because we are destroying our natural resources at a geometrically increasing rate. Once we put into motion an electromagnetic energy system, it will be self-sustaining. We must drop the veil of secrecy about UFOs and their advanced technologies, thereby creating a new global perspective, a new mindset for the entire planet. We can't wait anymore; we have to do it now.

Disclosure is about the truth, and now is the time for it. Up to 1993, I felt it was my duty to maintain the oath I took, promising not to divulge classified information on UFOs and UFO technology. Life with a Cosmos clearance means a person has the knowledge that UFOs exist. Air Force Intelligence, CIA, NRO and Naval Intelligence—even the FBI—were all involved in UFO investigations at Langley Field, Virginia. I worked in the cryptographics center, which is where all the encoded messages are sent. That, of course, is a Top Secret division of the government. U.S. Marines guard the code rooms where cryptographics are kept, whether in embassies, military bases or elsewhere.

There are about thirty-eight levels of classified clearance above Top Secret. I worked within the highest level of Cosmos clearance, which grants access to information about UFOs, extraterrestrials and *particlization* (converting waves into particles, or mass, as happens in the pineal gland of the human brain). There are probably only twenty-five people in the world who know the information at that level. No president of the U.S. has ever been cleared to that level. President Kennedy was the last president to have in-depth knowledge of UFOs, and President Eisenhower was the last to do anything about it, although other presidents knew about UFOs as well and made public statements about them.

During Eisenhower's era there were several intelligence agencies. The Army had an intelligence unit, as did the Air Force and the Navy. In addition, there were secret intelligence agencies. The one I worked for was so secret that it didn't exist. This agency, called the NRO, could never be mentioned; its name couldn't even be spoken aloud. For those on that level, there was also another worldwide group called the Advanced Contact Intelligence Organization (ACIO). If you paid your dues and obeyed the rules, you could truly benefit from the information gathered by those government organizations. Some in the military refer to these groups as the Guardians of the High Frontier. I believe now that everyone in this world should be privy to what is known by these Top Secret organizations. This is why I have allowed this information to be published now.

All the military intelligence units worked together, and at one time, the various units and the NRO were all housed together in a certain facility at Langley Air Force Base. We all worked in one building, and information was released only to those with top clearance and a "need to know." Most of the satellite interpreters were there, as were most of the intelligence interpreters from the Air Force, the Army and the Navy. Ike was a military man, so he liked to have somebody in charge, someone who could be blamed if something went wrong. He first appointed the director of the CIA to head the NRO, but that didn't work out. The CIA was primarily working for itself, and most of the intelligence directors for the various services also worked for themselves. Eisenhower wanted the NRO to be independent, reporting only to the president. It was only after 1997 that its name was spoken or printed; it was never, under any circumstances, printed prior to that time. In fact, in 1968, this would become the Star Wars Intelligence Program.

At the beginning of World War II, the U.S. did not have a spy network like Germany and Britain did. Our first attempt to develop a network of spies was the creation of the Office of Strategic Services (OSS), which was composed mainly of soldier spies, men from certain parts of the military as well as the FBI and other law enforcement agencies.[3] It was also at this time that we developed our first spy planes—the U-2, the A-12 and the Blackbird.

I was not a spy, but with my cryptographic clearance I had access to all the information being gathered at Langley. I also had a high clearance because I was a chief Conrad courier. During both the hot and cold wars, a military warrant officer would carry a little bag that contained the war codes and accompany the president of the United States. Wherever he was, the president could at any time declare war, and in his capacity as commander in chief he would receive a new war code each day.

The war codes involved a two-man control system, all the way from the men with the president down to those at the missile launch systems on the bombers and submarines and missile silos. Every nuclear weapon was controlled by the president through that little bag carried by the warrant officer, who was never out of the president's presence. Being a courier was a two-man job. These two men carried the war codes at all times and transferred the codes to all commanders throughout the field. Sometimes the couriers would fly on civilian airplanes, but two armed men from a base would always meet them.

It was, of course, extremely important to transfer the war codes to the right persons. There would be surprise tests. Once the men had been properly identified, they would receive the war codes. These two men would return to their base, and the codes would then be distributed to the war rooms—to the commanders, the operations officers, whoever was in charge. If at any time there was a threat of war, the controllers at the radar towers for the fighter-bombers would have to verify that the message was truly from the president, so the controllers would break the seal on the code box. If it was authentic, the Secretary of Armed Forces (the Navy, the Army and the Air Force) would give orders to launch missiles.

My first official duty upon entering the Air Force involved radar systems. I was fortunate to work under a genius, a great mathematical genius of our time—Benoit Mandelbrot.[4] He converted the military's conventional Security Information System (SIF) to what became known as Mode-6 transponders. Originally our security system had been built from vacuum tubes, but he changed it to transistors and printed circuit boards. During World War II, this monitoring system was known as Identification Friend or Foe (IFF); after the war it became the Security Information Defense (SID). To the present day, every airplane that flies has a Mode-6 transponder on board. Before the conversion to this advanced system, security systems had to be transported by ship or by an airplane large enough to hold the huge vacuum-tube system. Today, military couriers can carry the security system in their hand, in a car, anywhere. The Mode-6 transponder, along with the infamous "black box," is the first item looked for after a crash. When it is found, its contents can reveal why the airplane crashed and what went wrong with the navigation.

✳   ✳   ✳

It was in the Air Force that I discovered, in my official capacity, that there were UFOs and ETs. I did for Air Force Intelligence what William Cooper did for Navy Intelligence, which involved UFOs and cover-ups. We often exchanged information and data and were well aware of MAJI. MJ-12 is Majestic 12 (later Majesty 12), the official UFO policy group that had been formed after the Roswell UFO crash in 1947. Operation Majestic 12 was established by special classified presidential order at the urgency of the then Secretary of Defense James V. Forrestal (who, among others, was put in charge of MJ-12) and Dr. Vannevar Bush, chairman of the Joint Research and Development Board at that time. Forrestal was later thrown out the window of the National Naval Medical Center in Bethesda near Washington, D.C. The fall did not kill him, but he never got up off the ground. He lost his life because he had wanted to open the UFO files to the public after he'd visited and interviewed an extraterrestrial biological entity at a highly secured facility.

MJ-12 operations were carried out under a top-secret research program reporting only to the president. The goal of MJ-12 was the recovery, for scientific study, of all materials and devices of extraterrestrial manufacture as well as all biological entities and remains of entities. The CIA really grew out of the

MJ-12 policy group, because its initial purpose was to monitor the extraterrestrial "problem." MJ-12 established and administered special, secure facilities located at secret bases in the United States, bases that had been specially created to receive and process any material or entities classified as being of extraterrestrial origin. Of greatest interest for MJ-12 was the advanced technology.

I was officially active in the military Project Blue Book, which was designed to cover up the UFO problem. I was a member of the first team sent to investigate UFO sightings. I would talk to a witness as a military official in order to convince the person that he or she had not really seen anything unusual. If I could not sway the witness, then the number two team would go in and threaten the witness and family. If that team did not achieve its goal, the "OO-Boys" would be sent, and that would be the end of that—one way or another.

By 1947, we knew that our powerful radar (one to five million megawatts of radiated energy) could interfere with the navigation of extraterrestrial spacecraft. Where do we have our most powerful radar? In White Sands, New Mexico. When the UFOs crashed near Roswell, we had been tracking them at White Sands with our radar. One craft was completely destroyed; the other contained three beings, who were taken to secured facilities. I believe there was a botanist, Dr. Guillermo Mendoza, who worked with the survivors, because they took energy from the Sun like a plant. Their systems, however, could not survive in this environment. The UFOs sighted over Washington, D.C., in the early 1950s was their command group coming to announce their presence to the world.

We have been working with extraterrestrial technology since World War II, when we first learned that the Germans had developed advanced UFO technology. At that time, it wasn't called UFO technology; it was an electromagnetic antigravitational propulsion system.

One of my first personal experiences of a UFO, in an official capacity, happened in 1949 when I was stationed at Warner Robbins Air Force Base in Georgia. The command had sent me and my team of five men to where the Strategic Air Command (SAC) was testing whether they could penetrate our radar screen. Even the commander of the base did not know we were there with our powerful radar system, the FPS-5 and FPS-4. We got our equipment set up and operating, with three men on the tower and two down on control. We were in a building that had French doors along one side so that we could set up our radarscope.

One of the men said, "Look, a UFO!" Nobody turned around to look, because that was when Project Blue Book had begun to debunk UFO sightings (this was prior to my becoming a member of the Blue Book team). We all knew that if you said you had seen a UFO, it got complicated. Someone else then said to turn around and look, so we did. I could see three silver UFOs sitting in the atmosphere about a half mile from the tower. We asked each other what we would say if Dr. J. Allen Hynek came up here. Hynek was a distinguished astrophysicist and head of Ohio State University's astronomy department. He had been contracted to sort out all UFO reports for the Air Force. His official answer to a sighting was always autosuggestion, mass hypnosis or swamp gas. None of those craft show up on radar, so we went down to the control and turned on that radar.

On the base at that time were twenty thousand civilians and at least ten thousand military personnel, so we figured somebody else had to have seen those UFOs. I called headquarters to notify them: "We have contact." They asked if SAC was running a mission against us, which is how SAC tested our radar capabilities. I told them that it was not SAC, it was Cosmos. The commander told me to throw the switch to scramble the phone, then asked what I meant by saying we had Cosmos contact.

Fig. 3. A UFO radar photo taken at Warner Robbins Air Force Base.

"There are three UFOs sitting outside the tower!" I said. He told us to take photos and radar pictures and not to say another word. We got out official Air Force cameras and went outside and photographed the UFOs. We also took pictures with radar cameras. A courier arrived five or six hours later, by which time we had everything sealed up, and took the package back to the Eglin Air Force Proving Ground. We never received a memo confirming the receipt of those photos, not a word; it was as if the sighting had never happened. But I had copies of the pictures and gave each man on my team a photo as a keepsake for his grandchildren.

This experience prompted our interest in UFOs. We had personally witnessed these spacecraft, which was better than merely seeing radarscopes or registered information from the cryptographic center, and we had pictures to prove it.

What we refer to in Cosmos intelligence as Orion technology is an extraterrestrial technology that is at least 250 years ahead of ours. It really is like the film *Star Wars*. In the military I learned that we have already made contact with four other planets in this universe. I believe we have a responsibility to tell all the people about this; otherwise we are bypassing the Constitution of the United States.

The secret military intelligence units have carried this knowledge since 1947. There are far too many Black Projects going on, none of which is approved by Congress and all of which are funded by taxpayers' money. The American people have the right to know what their government is spending their money on and a right to benefit from technologies that have existed here for such a long time. If we don't break the secrecy surrounding our contact with extraterrestrial races and their advanced technology, we are doing ourselves great harm.

So why hasn't the existence of UFOs and extraterrestrial visitors been made public? The real problem rests with the fossil fuel energy industries. *We already have the technology for free energy*—the electromagnetic propulsion system, which will make everything else obsolete. The government sees the transition from dependence on oil to ET technology as a time of great danger, a time when oil stocks, industries, economies and governments could collapse. However, the extraterrestrials are going to force the hand of destiny. If we don't tell the public, they will. When they have made contact with enough people, they will reveal this information.

So again, who really is the enemy? Some would like us to believe the extraterrestrial peoples are the enemy. I want to assure people that we have nothing to fear from them. This is the purpose of the Disclosure Project led by Steven Greer, and we who are retired from military, civilian and other agencies from around the world have proved it.

Eisenhower, who personally met with an ambassador from another planet, warned the public not to let the military and industrial weapon builders take control. He always feared that. If you read his last speech to Congress, you will see these words:

> In the councils of government, we must guard against the acquisition of unwarranted influence, whether sought or unsought, by the military-industrial complex. The potential for the disastrous rise of this misplaced power exists and will persist.
>
> We must never let the weight of this combination endanger our liberties or democratic processes. We should take nothing for granted. Only an alert and knowledgeable citizenry can compel the proper meshing of the huge industrial and military machinery of defense with our peaceful methods and goals, so that security and liberty may prosper together.[5]

We knowingly and unknowingly live in the presence of extraterrestrial intelligence every day, a truth to which we must awaken. The consequence of remaining in ignorance is to allow decisions regarding these visitors and ourselves to be made by others.

Notes

1. This two-video documentary is available through the Disclosure Project Web page at www.disclosureproject.org. A printed version containing many more testimonies is also available at www.lighttechnology.com. See also Steven M. Greer, M.D., *Disclosure: Military and Government Witnesses Reveal the Greatest Secrets in Modern History* (Crozet, Va.: Crossing Point, Inc., 2001). These testimonies were transcribed from taped interviews of over four hundred witnesses.
2. William Cooper, *Behold a Pale Horse* (Flagstaff, Ariz.: Light Technology Publishing, 1991). www.lighttechnology.com

3. For more information, see Bruce S. Maccabee, Ph.D., *The UFO-FBI Connection* (St. Paul: Llewellyn Publications, 2000) and Nick Redfern, *The FBI Files: The FBI's UFO Top Secrets Exposed* (London: Simon & Schuster, 1999).

4. For more information on Benoit Mandelbrot, see the following films: *Fractals: The Color of Infinity,* directed by Nigel Lesmoir-Gordon, 54 min., 1994, videocassette; and *Dan Salter UFO File II*, produced by Daniel M. Salter, 120 min., 1995, videocassette, Red Star Productions.

5 President Dwight D. Eisenhower, "Farewell Radio and Television Address to the American People," January 17, 1961, http://eisenhower.archives.gov/farewell.htm.

CHAPTER TWO

WEAPONIZING SPACE

The National Security Agency (NSA) is really in charge of how much UFO information is going to be released. In 1969, I was transferred from the Air Force Intelligence to the National Reconnaissance Office (NRO) at Langley Air Force Base in Virginia, where I worked at the headquarters of the Interplanetary Phenomenon Scientific and Technical Intelligence Unit, in the counterintelligence unit. My specific duty was to investigate UFOs, aliens and particlization. The NRO was part of the CIA, but if you worked for the CIA, you worked for a different organization. If you saw the film *Enemy of*

Fig. 4. License plate for the NRO counterintelligence unit.

the State, you know that the NRO spies on everybody. That should give you an idea of the state of mind of the people who keep these secrets.

During the Cold War, the Star Wars project was originally a U.S. missile defense system, but that was a smoke screen for putting weapons into space. During the Disclosure Project Press Conference in Washington, D.C., I met and talked with Dr. Carol Rosin, who spoke with great eloquence on this subject.[1] She was the first woman manager for Fairchild Industries. She was also the spokesperson for Wernher von Braun in his later years. Von Braun was a missile expert we imported from Germany in 1946, after World War II. The U.S. and the Russians imported many leading scientists and technicians during Project Paperclip. Von Braun had been the leader of the Nazis' missile program and the U.S. wanted him because we were having a hard time launching our rockets. After we put von Braun in charge, the program was a success.

Dr. Rosin worked for von Braun until his death. He would frequently tell her that she had to inform people after he was gone that he'd been against putting missiles into space. He knew that the U.S. Deep Space Intelligence Headquarters would use these weapons against the extraterrestrials and that it would be to humanity's detriment. Von Braun knew that from 1947 through 1951, we had shot down, captured and arrested extraterrestrials with their vehicles so we could study them. Yet the ETs have never committed an aggressive act toward humans; humans have always shot first. Once the U.S. put missiles into space, it was bound to use them, for America has *always* used the weapons it has built.

Around 1962, during President Kennedy's administration, the U.S. Air Force launched a missile with a nuclear warhead to the Moon. We had put our first probe on the Moon, with attendant publicity, in 1959. Now we were secretly planning to explode a nuclear missile there just to see what would happen. However, it was shot down by a UFO that came up behind it, fired a pulse-beam weapon at it, then pulled up beside it and fired again. Then it pulled in front and fired at the nose, the location of the nuclear warhead, went to the other side and fired again. So the UFO knocked out the U.S. Air Force's missile and deflected its path. Luckily, we were never able to detonate that or any other nuclear warhead on the Moon.

The Disclosure Project has identified hundreds of military, intelligence, government and corporate witnesses of this and other phenomena.

Testimony of Dr. Carol Rosin, December 2000:

> What was most interesting to me was a repetitive sentence that he [Wernher von Braun] said to me over and over again during the approximately four years that I had the opportunity to work with him. He said the strategy that was being used to educate the public and decision makers was to use scare tactics. . . . That was how we identify an enemy.
>
> The strategy that Werner [sic] von Braun taught me was that first the Russians are going to be considered to be the enemy. . . . Then terrorists would be identified. . . . Then we were going to identify third-world "crazies.". . . The next enemy was asteroids. Now, at this point he kind of chuckled the first time he said it. . . .
>
> And the funniest one of all was what he called aliens, extraterrestrials. That would be the final scare. And over and over . . . he would bring up that last card. "And remember Carol, the last card is the alien card. We are going to have to build space-based weapons against aliens and all of it is a lie." [2]

※   ※   ※

Testimony of Colonel Ross Dedrickson, U.S. Air Force (ret.)/AEC, September 2000:

And then further on I finally retired from the Air Force and joined the Boeing Company where I was assigned to the Minute Man program where I was responsible for the accounting of all the nuclear fleet, the Minute Man One, Two, and Three. And during that period of time, I also learned about incidents involving nuclear weapons. And among these incidents were those where a couple of nuclear weapons that were sent into space were destroyed by the extraterrestrials. . . .

. . . There was for example, a Minute Man missile that was destroyed after a launch from Vandenberg Air Force Base. That's now a public matter of record. In this incident, they actually photographed the UFO following the missile as it climbed into space and, shining a beam on it, neutralized the missile. . . .

. . . It was my understanding that in either the very end of the '70s or the early '80s that we attempted to put a nuclear weapon on the Moon and explode it for scientific measurements and other things which was not acceptable to the extraterrestrials. . . .

The ETs destroyed the weapon as it went toward the Moon. The idea of any explosion of a nuclear weapon in space by any Earth government was not acceptable to the extraterrestrials and that has been demonstrated over and over.[3]

※   ※   ※

Testimony of Professor Robert Jacobs, Lt. U.S. Air Force, November 2000:

We were testing ballistic missiles that were to deliver nuclear weapons on target . . . it was my duty to supervise the instrumentation photography of every missile that went down in that western test range. . . .

. . . and into the frame came something else. It flew into the frame like and it shot a beam of light at the warhead.

Now remember, all this stuff is flying at several thousand miles an hour. So this thing [UFO] fires a beam of light at the warhead, hits it. . . . and the warhead tumbles out of space. The object, the points of light that we saw, the warhead and so forth, were traveling through subspace about 60 miles straight up. And they were going somewhere in the neighborhood of 11,000 to 14,000 miles an hour when this UFO caught up to them, flew in, flew around them, and flew back out.[4]

※   ※   ※

The testimony of Capt. Robert Salas, U.S. Air Force, December 2000, [is about an incident]: "On the morning of March 16, 1967 . . . 16 nuclear missiles simultaneously became non-operational at two different launch facilities immediately after guards saw UFOs hovering above. The guards could not identify these objects even though they were only about 30 feet away. The Air Force did an intensive investigation of the incidents and could not find a probable cause." [5]

✳   ✳   ✳

Testimony of Mr. Harland Bentley, August 2000:

> I have been in a graduate program for nuclear engineering
> . . . and have been working contracts since 1963: NASA, Department
> of Energy and several other electronics firms in the Washington,
> D.C. area. . . .
>
> . . . I was at a facility in California, that is all I can say, and I
> was doing particular classified work . . . at the same time that our
> astronauts were doing a loop around the moon and back again. . . .
> I heard them say they had a bogey (term used for unknown target,
> and often specifically used to denote a UFO) coming in at 11:00. . . .
>
> It was another type of ship. There were portals there that they
> could see in. They could see beings of some sort. They did not
> describe these beings. They just took photographs. . . . They just said
> it was a saucer shaped craft. . . . Then they said, "There they go." And
> they [the bogey] went out of sight almost immediately . . . .[6]

The extraterrestrials' directive to the inhabitants of planet Earth was not to use nuclear weapons in space. They essentially told the U.S. and the Russians that they would not put up with it. However, much later, in 1995, France tested its own nuclear weapons in the South Pacific near Tahiti and blew a hole in the Earth's mantle. In their ignorance, they precipitated profound changes in the world climate and created a hole in the ozone layer over the Antarctic. The extraterrestrials apparently know how humans think and had thus warned us years earlier so we would avoid such unintended consequences.

The extraterrestrials finally convinced the U.S. to stop using nuclear weapons in space, but where do you think our spare nuclear weapons went? The U.S. and Russia parked them in space as a first line of defense! Those nuclear weapons are still up there today. World leaders wonder why the extraterrestrials come here and what they want; they are suspicious of their motives. In the face of those fears, our response has been to weaponize space. Military minds figured that if the extraterrestrials became aggressive, the military would blow them up, but the ETs have proven that they can render our weapons harmless.

✳   ✳   ✳

In July 1969, the first Apollo Moon Mission was followed by a nonterrestrial spacecraft. In fact, the astronauts took pictures of it all the way up. After they landed, there were three UFOs sitting there. It was years before NASA would release those photos—not to the public but to the scientists, administrators and engineers who were involved in the Moon exploration project.

The extraterrestrials have an aboveground facility on the dark side of the Moon, which is always faced away from Earth telescopes; I have read NASA reports about this base. Photos taken by one of our Moon-orbiting satellites show visible structures under what appear to be three glass biospheres. I and other researchers have seen films of the bridges and roads inside the domed structures. From 1968 to 1969, during the time when the U.S. tried to establish a secret base on the Moon, astronauts filmed this area without NASA's permission. Their photos clearly show a collapsed structure inside the biosphere. The dome literally collapsed; you could see only some walkways.

I have read NASA reports that when the U.S. landed to establish this secret base on the Moon, they tried to take over that ET facility, which they had detected through signals that could only have been those of a power station. During that same timeline, in the late 1980s, we were told by extraterrestrials not to interfere with that Moon base; it belonged to another civilization that would be coming back to use it. When the ET vessel approached the U.S.'s landing vehicle, they did not destroy it because their advanced sensors told them the American astronauts would not fire on them. They simply rendered the lander inoperable by using a pulse-beam weapon, informing us again not to send another craft. The U.S. nevertheless sent two more missions to the Moon in the early 1990s, but they were also destroyed. A third was launched to obtain better resolution than our Moon orbiter, but it was destroyed in transit. We eventually wised up, and NASA abandoned further manned Moon landings.

The Russians were given the same warning. Russian photographs recovered in the late 1980s show a strange extraterrestrial vehicle moving toward one of their craft. The Russians fired a probe beam toward the extraterrestrial spacecraft, and it responded by destroying the Russian vessel. The Russians subsequently tried to send three more lunar craft, but two of them never got off the ground; the third was destroyed in space.

It was during this period that in a speech to the United Nations General Assembly in its forty-second session, President Ronald Reagan said:

> In our obsession with antagonisms of the moment, we often forget how much unites all the members of humanity. Perhaps we need some outside, universal threat to make us realize this common bond. I occasionally think how quickly our differences worldwide would vanish if we were facing an alien threat from outside this world. And yet, I ask you, is not an alien force already among us?"[7]

Earlier, in remarks to Fallston High School students and faculty in Fallston, Maryland, President Reagan talked about a recent meeting with General Secretary Mikhail Gorbachev:

> When you stop to think that we're all God's children, wherever we may live in the world . . . just think how easy his [Gorbachev's] task and mine might be . . . if suddenly there was a threat . . . from some other species from another planet outside the universe. We'd forget all the little local differences . . . and we would find out once and for all that we really are all human beings here on this earth together.[8]

I estimate that we have known of an extraterrestrial presence on the Moon for at least fifty years. NASA will no longer let astronauts film anything from the space capsule. And because their transmissions have been picked up by U.S. citizens, NASA switches to a secure broadcast frequency whenever the astronauts begin to report anomalies.

Some people believe that Americans never landed on the Moon. They think it all took place on a back lot of some movie studio. This idea, though not new, was discussed in late summer 2001 by Katie Couric on NBC's *Today Show* in New York City. She showed a film segment speculating whether or not U.S. astronauts ever went to the Moon. Of course, this is deliberate disinformation to counter the facts of extraterrestrial contact and is a part of the government's secrecy campaign. That story was concocted so that nobody would believe we had contact with extraterrestrials and UFOs on our first Moon mission. The spin doctors know how to create confusion so that people won't know what is really going on.

In the early 1990s, Giorgio Bongiovanni, the Italian stigmatist, went to Russia three times to convince the Russians to surrender their secret files and documents concerning their astronauts' experiences with UFOs when in their sky labs. He brought much of this documentation to Washington in 1995 and asked officials, "How are you going to match this?" Under this pressure, NASA had to release a lot of information, some of which is in the Library of Congress and in media archives.

I believe that the government has made deals with certain people to create specific messages about UFOs and extraterrestrials in films, television, articles and books and allowed them to view microfilm from classified and declassified archives. Take, for example, Steven Spielberg's *Close Encounters of the Third Kind*. This film is ambiguous enough to be either believed or disbelieved, depending on the viewer's bias. The government guarantees that if such a film loses money, it will pay the difference. To date it has never had to do that.

The Orson Welles broadcast of H.G. Wells' "The War of the Worlds" in 1938 was dramatically presented as a live news report. Taking it as factual, the public panicked, which contributed to the government's later decision to cover up the facts about extraterrestrial contact. But the H.G. Wells story also reflects humanity's fear of the unknown and of those unlike ourselves.

This secret government has enlisted the media as a partner in keeping the truth from the public by its silence, ridicule, disinformation or misdirection. Its purpose is to weaponize space for a mock invasion, something similar to an *Independence Day* scenario. Using the media, the government is preparing people for this sort of event. They are preparing for a major "disclosure"— which will be a monumental hoax—that our real enemy is the ETs. The truth is that the enemy is really ourselves and our secret government. If that weren't so, we wouldn't have been so easy to manipulate—and the secret government would release the technologies that have been developed from back-engineered extraterrestrial spaceships. The zero-gravity system the government possesses harnesses free energy, which can save our ecosystems, our planet and all its life forms, and ultimately the solar system and worlds beyond.

The *X-Files*, a television program about the FBI for which producer Chris Carter was also allowed to view secured UFO documents, has conditioned the world to become familiar with these ideas. And now the CIA has created its own program in *The Agency*, first aired by CBS in October 2001. As the *New York Times* reported on May 6, 2001:

> Central Intelligence Agency headquarters is a sleepy place most weekends, but one recent Saturday it was forced to call in dozens of reinforcements to stave off a 20-hour siege.
>
> The invasion was not mounted by Iraqis, North Koreans or terrorists with phony passports but by CBS. . . .
>
> CBS is deep into filming a pilot for a series this fall that would tell stories of everyday life inside "The Agency." So it is understandable that CBS producers wanted to film opening scenes at the agency's headquarters in Langley, Va. . . .
>
> As part of its new mission, the C.I.A. is working regularly with filmmakers, television producers and writers it considers sympathetic.
>
> By doing so, it hopes both to get out what it calls the truth about the agency and to explain to a skeptical public why, in the absence of an overarching national enemy, it needs a budget of about $30 billion a year for its operations and those of its sister intelligence agencies.
>
> The C.I.A. is picky about its projects. . . . Bill Harlow, the agency's chief spokesman . . . [says]: "If they appear to be interested in accuracy, if they do not misportray the role of the agency, and we can do so without interfering with our mission, we will consider providing assistance."[9]

The CIA has conditioned the public about its role for many years, with cover-ups and deep secrets. We will soon see what their agenda is. *The Agency* may try to explain what the CIA has done with the extraterrestrials—but if they don't, they have been warned. If they don't get the public ready for disclosure and try to raise the level of consciousness concerning humanity's place in the solar system and the galaxy, the extraterrestrials will do it.

The problem lies in the secret government's agenda for weaponizing space. How did Hitler prepare the German people for war? He had to create fear, then set up a scapegoat to blame. He also created the concept of a new world order, and this has been adopted by our government as a symbol of its complete control. At the same time this secret government is pursuing its agenda of fear, the extraterrestrials are raising the consciousness of humanity through contact, dreams, sightings, telepathy and paranormal experiences. The ultimate purpose of both is to change human consciousness—one through engendering fear and the other through loosening the hold of the current worldview, allowing humanity to make a spiritual shift and thus ready itself for a future dimensional change.

The Mayan calendar says that by 2012, the era of the Fifth Sun will begin. Biblical prophecies about the "end times" are expected to be completed one way or another; the Hopi are waiting for the return of the True White Brother. Unless we wake up and take our place among other cosmic civilizations, we will miss entering the prophesied thousand years of peace. As our governments begin to lose control over us, human consciousness is awakening to the fact that we are not alone in the cosmos. We are close to making an evolutionary leap and becoming citizens of the universe.

The Vatican and Pope John Paul II believe enough in UFOs to have formed a committee of bishops in 1992 to study secret documents that are for insider eyes only. They have put one of the most powerful telescopes in the world on Mount Graham, on the San Carlos Apache Reservation in Arizona, to keep an eye on what's going on in outer space. They know that the knowledge of extraterrestrial civilizations would shake the foundation of religious belief, which is tied into the economics of world power.

By presidential order it is a federal offense for a private citizen to communicate with extraterrestrials. The "Men in Black" are real; they are agents for a certain part of our government. "Our government" is a broad term for a very select group, one who does not report to the president. As stated by Senator Daniel K. Inouye, "There exists a shadowy Government with it's [sic] own Air Force, its own Navy, it's [sic] own fundraising mechanism, and the ability to pursue its own ideas of the national interest, free from all checks and balances, and free from the law itself."[10] They are at the helm of our ship of state. The Men in Black discourage people from reporting what they have seen. If they are unsuccessful, the OO-Boys and the Wackenhut assassins are called in. I know this firsthand. In the Disclosure Project, many testimonies of the military men concerned their experiences with these OO-Boys, none of which were pleasant. They are also known as the "1010" and the "54-12 Men."

In the past, all these people reported to MAJI and the president, but they began to keep the president out of the loop. The Men in Black have been in charge of keeping Area 51 secret all these years. Signs there warn you that trespassers face deadly force. That deadly force are the Wackenhut security people. They are killers, but other agencies terminate people as well. This sort of thing took place under Project Grudge, Project Sign, Project Bear and Project Blue Book. Military people who witnessed UFO activity, heard in a wide variety of testimonies, were the easiest to control; however, they had little power over extraterrestrials. The ETs, advanced far beyond our civilization, have the technology to protect themselves, with occasional exceptions, and interfere with our power sources if they choose.

❋　　　　　❋　　　　　❋

In ancient Eastern texts such as the *Ramayana*, the *Bhagavad Gita* and the Koran, there are passages that describe a nuclear war. In these accounts, dreadful weapons burned people's images into the ground, just like at Hiroshima, and permanently poisoned the soil. Lord Desmond Leslie, the nephew of Winston Churchill, studied these texts at great length, and in *Flying Saucers Have Landed* he noted what they said about extraterrestrials, sky travel and sky wars. He wrote of a destroyed civilization that had airships with beings from heaven who came to Earth. This time period was from fifty thousand to one hundred thousand years ago.[11]

Among the Earth-based peoples of this planet are records on stone depicting sky travel. In Brazil, Colombia, the sub-Sahara, Australia and even North America, indigenous peoples say they come from another planetary system. The Dogon tribe in Africa and the Aborigines of Australia both claim to be descendants of beings from the planet Sirius. There are rock "art galleries" in Australia dating back fifty thousand years that depict flying aircraft and unusual beings. In the northwestern and central Kimberley region of Western Australia is the oldest surviving art form, and one at a site in the Northern Territory is dated thirty-four thousand years in the past. The drawings depict flying aircraft and unusual looking beings.

Scientists and researchers who talked to the Dogon tribe were amazed at the knowledge this tribe had of Sirius. Before the invention of the telescope, the Dogon knew that Sirius had a dark star and later another star. How did the ancient peoples know this? Where are they actually from? And above all, how did they get here?

© by Nqarinyin.

Fig. 5. "Ancestral Being Wandjina" by Nqarinyin.

The Aboriginal people of Australia experience what they call the Dreamtime, which is a literal dimension. We have forgotten it, but now we are paying more attention to what is called Dreamtime. Our scientists are studying what the Aboriginals mean by it and what they do there. We know it is possible for them to be seen in two places at once, and they say they can move backward and forward in historical time.

Most children born after 1988 or 1989, the children of the Woodstock generation, diverted the path humanity was taking. Their parents had made a spiritual breakthrough that passed to their children. These children are different. Doctors have discovered and science has proven some definitive differences. In *The Urantia Book*, which I taught for many years at Mountain View College in Dallas, Texas, these children are called *Homo erectus, Serapian*. Most of these kids are spiritual-minded and have more knowledge at birth than did their parents.

The children of today won't take their parents' word for things. They intuitively know the truth despite the distorted history they are taught. Their body temperature is often up to two degrees above normal, and some have extra vertebrae in the tailbone. They often suffer from asthma and have breathing difficulties. Most of these kids have had their tonsils and adenoids removed and are sometimes highly sensitive to viruses. But this generation knows that we are not the only inhabitants of our galaxy. When the extraterrestrials make contact, they will take it in stride.

The children of this world are our future; their generation will change the way we live. That is another reason we should release the secrets and disclose the truth; we otherwise harm future generations. The children are far more advanced than their parents or professors. Even today they stand up and say, "No, that's not the way it is; that's not the way it was!" They are like a lost tribe wandering around. Instead of teaching the history of humanity, we should be teaching the history of extraterrestrials and their advanced technology. These children know the truth; they are born knowing it. Some have lost hope because they have been filled with untruths and idiocies. Our children would be inspired by knowledge of the real truth of extraterrestrial worlds and the evolution of our human spirit. We should have a program for studying higher cosmic knowledge and ET civilizations.

I'm convinced that somehow about 10 percent of humans will wake up one morning and say, "I know this!" Maybe human consciousness will rise through osmosis. I think it's taking place now, and that's exciting to me. By continuing the secrecy, we are doing humanity a great disservice. Instead of our president talking about education and testing, we need to teach the truth about other civilizations we have made contact with. That is why I am breaking this oath of secrecy—for the "seventh generation," those who come after us.

Notes

1. Rosin founded the Institute for Cooperation in Space, headquartered in Washington, D.C., and has often testified before Congress concerning space-based weapons.
2. Steven M. Greer, M.D., *Disclosure: Military and Government Witnesses Reveal the Greatest Secrets in Modern History* (Crozet, Va.: Crossing Point, Inc., 2001), 255–256.
3. Ibid., 192–193.
4. Ibid., 183–184.
5. Ibid., 167.
6. Ibid., 429, 431.
7. http://www.qtm.net/~geibdan/newsa/reagan.html.
8. http://www.reagan.utexas.edu/resource/speeches/1985/120485a.htm.
9. Elaine Sciolino, "Cameras Are Being Turned on a Once-Shy Spy Agency," *New York Times*, 6 May 2001, Travel Section.
10. Greer, *Disclosure*, 1.
11. Desmond Leslie and George Adamski, *Flying Saucers Have Landed* (New York: The British Book Centre, 1953). For more information, see 1995 *Dan Salter UFO File III*, produced by Daniel M. Salter, 120 min., 1995, videocassette, Red Star Productions.

CHAPTER THREE

THE KALAHARI RETRIEVALS

Official military documents indicate that a sixty-foot spacecraft entered South African airspace at 1:45 P.M. on May 7, 1989, and was intercepted by two Mirage jet fighters using an experimental laser cannon. This caused the spacecraft to crash in the Kalahari Desert, creating a crater four hundred feet wide and thirty-six feet deep. The craft and its two surviving extraterrestrial crew members were removed to a secret air force base. A retrieval team came from the United States, and a C-5 Galaxy transport vehicle took the craft and the two extraterrestrial beings back to Wright-Patterson Air Force Base in Dayton, Ohio.

The spacecraft commander, Akon, had for many years been visiting a South African woman named Elizabeth Klarer. The South African Air Force had often seen this craft, and the United States military had been made aware of it. The South Africans have a small air force, but it is very efficient because they have French Mirages. I'm not sure if

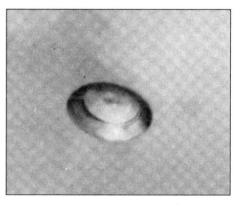

Fig. 6. Akon's spaceship.[1]

the Mirages laid in wait for the craft's arrival; however, they expected its return.

The Mirages intercepted the craft and transmitted warnings, but there was no response. The controllers on the ground told the pilot to use a laser weapon, which had been given to the South African Air Force by the United States government. (This is one of the secrets that Wen Ho Lee was recently accused of giving to Taiwan: antigravitational electromagnetic propulsion and pulse-beam laser weaponry. During the televised Senate hearings, the investigating committee chairman addressed the entire Senate, stating exactly what Lee had given away, thereby telling the world that we had a pulse-beam weapon. He was quickly shut up, and after that nobody talked. The fifty-nine charges against Lee were dropped to one and Lee was freed.)

The crash in South Africa was the first time that we recovered a complete spacecraft of extraterrestrial technology all in one piece. When the South African Air Force shot down the spacecraft with our laser weaponry, it was damaged only enough to force it to land. The ground controller had ordered the pilot to disable the craft and shoot it down, after which helicopters and ground troops came in. They picked up the craft and moved it to a secret base. After examining the exterior, the South Africans called the U.S. government. Upon investigation they found a crack in the door seam and opened it with hydraulic pumping gear. When they entered the craft, they found two beings and immediately took them into custody; one was injured and was removed to a medical facility in South Africa, where they did what they could for him. They also discovered symbols. To my knowledge, this was the first time an extraterrestrial written language had been recovered.

The U.S. was asked whether we wanted the ship, for we had given the South Africans the pulse-beam weapon that had brought it down. The U.S. military arrived three to five days later. The South African government made a deal with the U.S. that if they gave us everything they had retrieved from the crash, we would support them when they exploded their first atomic bomb and wouldn't protest it at the United Nations. The rest of the world might criticize them about their atomic weapons, but we couldn't say a thing. The U.S. agreed. From reports I have seen, it is my understanding that two U.S. C-5 Galaxy transports took the craft and the two beings, who were still alive, to Wright-Patterson Air Force Base, where most of the ET recoveries were taken at that time.

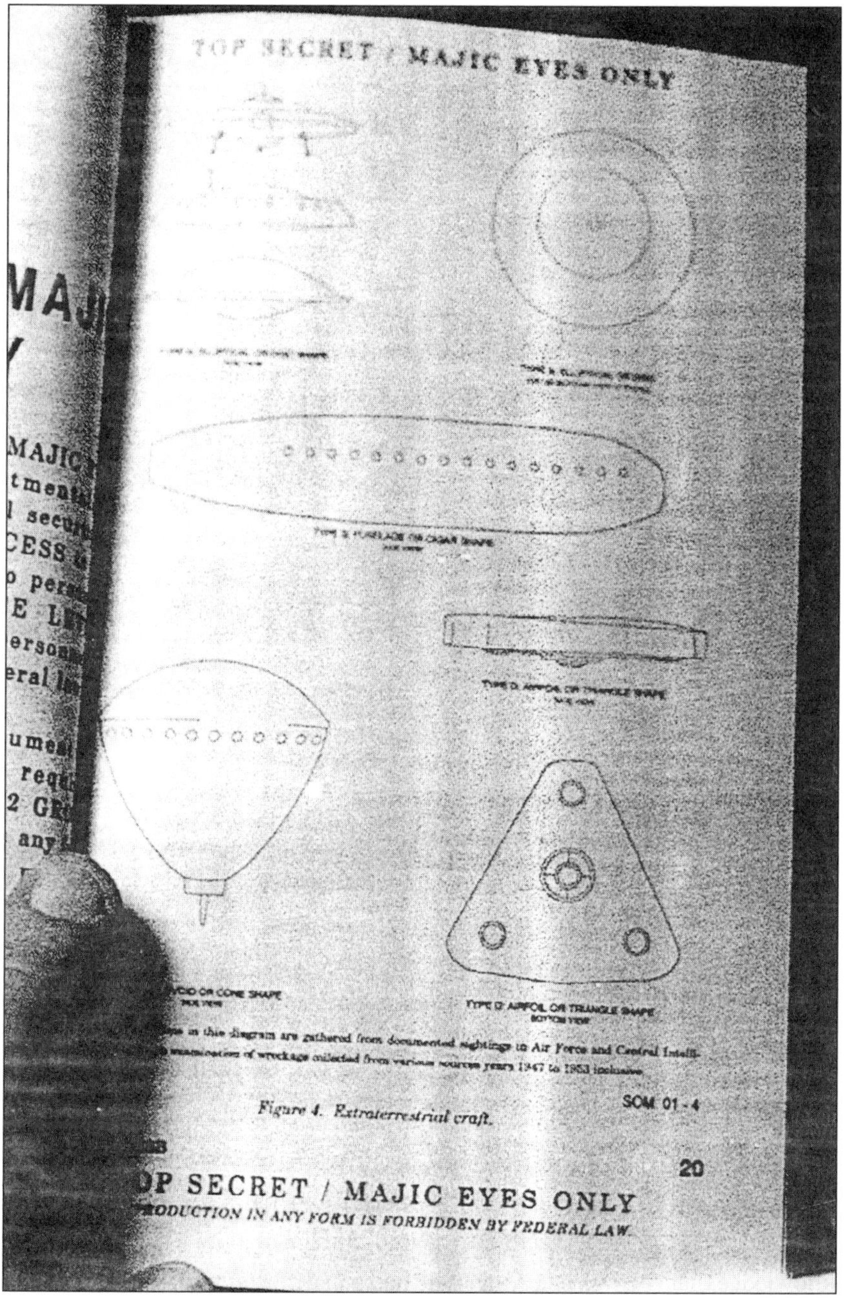

Fig. 7. UFO wrecking chart. Images in this diagram are gathered from documented sightings sent to the Air Force and the Central Intelligence Agency.

Fig. 8. Karl L. Veit, President of Duist Weisbaden, presenting Elizabeth Klarer with flowers after her talk at the Congress.[2]

Once we recovered this symbolic language, we tried to translate the language into something we could understand. However, our language is not like theirs, so there are a lot of symbols we can't decipher yet. The symbols have been seen before—in fact, one wall inside the Great Pyramid is covered with them. We have people secretly studying that language from the Great Pyramid.

❋   ❋   ❋

Elizabeth Klarer, born in 1910, was trained as an astronomer and was well educated. These extraterrestrial visits occurred from 1954 until her death in 1994. She tried to tell the world about her experiences, but at first many nations would not let her lecture. She told humanity about a higher scientific knowledge that she was receiving. She had an advanced understanding of the structure of the cosmos and the laws of light frequency that could have benefited humanity, science and our environment:

'The road to the stars unfolds within a spaceship of great beauty and simplicity, generating her light from the cosmic plasma of eternity, never faltering, always alive and pulsating, shaped like a galaxy with a halo surrounding her and the shock wave glowing.

'All of creation is light, the key to the Universe. The whole of existence throughout the planetary systems, the stars, the depths of interstellar space are all made up of visible and invisible waves of light . . . To the seen and unseen, to all energy, substance, liquids, gases and all life, the release of the microatoms of light from oxygen is the source of all life. The electromagnetic waveform, or Light. It forms the building blocks of the cosmos in which we have our being, as microatoms of light in greater unities are equal to atoms.

'Mind forces, spiritual strength, soul attainment and thoughts are all made up of different speeds in the wave-length of light, or microatoms. Electricity is microatoms of light while sound and colour occur when the microatoms have different speeds, and when microatoms are stopped, they create heat. Light is an intelligent energy which can be thought into existence and substance. The pattern of microatoms of light changes with changing thoughts, when one achieves the formula for the harmonic vibration of light.

'The key to all life and the Universe lies in harmonic interaction of light.

'A mathematical formula for all transportation lies in the vibratory frequencies of light harmonic, with anti-gravity waves and time waves, which are simply the frequency rate between each pulse of the spiral of light. By controlling this frequency rate, the flow of time can be varied, and one simply moves within one's environment within the protection of the spaceship instantaneously from one planet to another, or one solar system to another, where time, as a geometric, is controlled or eliminated.'[3]

Elizabeth Klarer was finally able to get this higher extraterrestrial knowledge to the world through books and lectures. She had been gifted, you might say, since birth. The cosmic visitors would come and take her to their planet. They opened doors for her with vast amounts of scientific information, which she eventually translated for humanity. The U.S. government knew about her and understood what she was saying. The scientific knowledge Klarer shared was three or four hundred years ahead of Earth's. I have read this in the documents pertaining to the Kalahari retrievals. The U.S.'s secret technology has made its greatest advances mostly because of these retrievals thirteen years ago. After the U.S. military began atomic bomb testing, the extraterrestrials told Klarer that if we continued, we would destroy our planet like they had theirs.

They had no government as such in their world, she told people, only a group of wise beings known as the Ancient Ones. Some people refer to such beings as avatars or even bodhisattvas.

Fig. 9. "Cosmic Visitors" by Christopher Schott.

I have spoken at length with Don Phillips, who also attended the Disclosure Project. He actually viewed the film footage of Eisenhower and the ET representative taken at an undisclosed site in California. Commander Graham E. Bethune says that the Orionites came to our planet in April of 1954 to what was at the time an air base called Muroc (now Edwards AFB), the supersecret Air Force test center in the high desert near Mojave, California. They met with President Eisenhower and through that meeting established contact between world governments and the Grays.

From the craft downed in South Africa, we built a lenticular vehicle that we could park six hundred miles out in space. (*Lenticular* refers to a beveled, triangular shape, sometimes called the Black Manta, which some people have seen.) The South African craft had no dashboard, throttle or wheel to control flight like we have; biocomputers allowed them to control the ship through their minds and through crystals. The controls before them looked like crystals. The computer read their minds for interstellar travel and was connected to a ship that circled our planet at a vast distance. We call it a mothership; to them it was central control.

The U.S. government's lenticular reentry vehicle is powered by electromagnetics. It has three engines: a jet engine to get out of the atmosphere and electric atomic engines it uses until it goes into warp speed for interplanetary travel. With electromagnetics we can travel faster than the speed of light. That type of engine literally pulls speed into the aircraft, or folds space. The U.S. has something like a biocomputer in this lenticular vehicle. If you check out the November 2000 issue of *Popular Mechanics*, you will be astounded to see a representation of this aircraft.[4] It carries enough nuclear weapons to wipe out Iraq and North Korea.

I believe that nonterrestrial governments are completely self-sufficient and have no monetary system. Everyone's needs are met, so there is no reason for a class system. This group of planetary citizens is referred to as a confederation but can be most aptly described as part of a supreme consciousness or mind. In our contacts with nonterrestrial beings, we would ask them, "Who's your God?" The answer has always been, "Everything. Everything there is." Earth's sacred literature has a similar teaching. We know that regardless of one's faith, all basic teachings stem from the same source.

※　　　　　※　　　　　※

We will all wind up—some of us kicking and screaming, some of us willingly—going through what Native Americans call the Void. Many of us accept that we are going from the third dimension to the fourth dimension, but Native American people think that we are going from the fourth to the fifth dimension. Having some Native American blood myself, I have studied those beliefs and teachings. I have spoken at length with the elders of the Hopi, Navajo, Tewa, Cherokee and Comanche, who shared this knowledge with me. To them, the fifth dimension is the Void. They believe that Void is an experience of life where life occurs instantaneously. What might take twenty-one years here would happen in two weeks there. One would have the knowledge of a twenty-one-year-old adult two weeks after birth. This is the Void, a literal dimension. When you think something, then it is.

We don't actually need a body; a lot of extraterrestrials do not materialize a body. They travel without a ship, through particlization. They need a ship only to protect themselves in different dimensions on different planets they visit. If they wish, they can materialize a spacecraft using materials that exist where they are traveling (though not to impress the creatures on the planets they are visiting). But they don't need a ship. They have been here many times without ships simply because *we* did not have them. What was the use, since they could just appear?

If you search the sacred texts and literature of many cultures and religions, you will find accounts of beings who have suddenly appeared. Angels and extraterrestrials are often indistinguishable. ETs can take the form of an angel that can be seen by us, or even the form of a kachina. They take the form of the cultural or religious figures of the people they visit so people can understand.

✳   ✳   ✳

Nobody knows exactly what happened to the two beings downed in South Africa who were taken to Wright-Patterson Air Force Base. I read in government files that we created a Faraday cage [named after Michael Faraday, the nineteenth-century physicist who proposed the first electromagnetic field theory], an electrified cage designed to keep the beings from walking through the walls. This was done because they can dematerialize their particles by changing their frequency to that of a wall, then move through the spaces between the particles. They can therefore come in and out of your home without using doors or windows. We have also created a biosphere glass dome/cage with a controlled atmosphere to allow extraterrestrial beings to survive for a limited amount of time. Neither the Faraday cage nor the glass dome could keep the beings alive for more than a year.

There was a nuclear war in the universe. The Grays' civilization in the Reticulum experienced a rebellion, a war that originated in the mind. To infect something in the universe, the Grays—like all living beings—first created it in the mind, where all disease begins. They came to Earth after destroying their civilization in order to learn a different way. They cannot breathe here; they have a hard time adjusting and cannot remain here for very long. If they do, they die before their time. A virus affects them and the light on Earth is too strong for them—that accounts for the dark shield over their eyes or, in some cases, their red eyes. (The red eyes provide protection from ultraviolet and infrared rays.) According to Don Phillips, a member of the Air Force and a CIA contractor, the "night vision" devices we have come from extraterrestrial technology derived from this black shield cover over their eyes. As Phillips testified, the Grays were born under a double star, where gravity is half of that on Earth. Everything they build is very light but exceedingly strong. Their foremost motive is exploration, and that is why they are studying the humans and also our environment:

> We have records from 1954 that were meetings between our own leaders of this country and ET's here in California. And, as I understand it from the written documentation, we were asked if we would allow them to be here and do research. I have read that our reply was, well, how can we stop you? You are so advanced. And I will say by this camera and this sound, that it was President Eisenhower that had this meeting. And it was on film, sort of like what we are doing now. Bringing it up to date, the NATO report gave that there were 12 races. To make a final summary, they had to have contacts to go to these races in order to understand who they are, what they are doing, and what they could do. And the report didn't get into the context, but it certainly did verify that they haven't been here for just a few years, but rather hundreds, maybe thousands of years. And, this is written in the text.
>
> Now, getting back to the ET technology that we might have used—the chips, lasers, the night vision, the bulletproof vests, and a few others—these were all developed. Well, the chips, what they call the central processing units, were developed in great strides. Now, why did that happen? Why, you put a few things together and do a bit of research, you think, wow—we did benefit.
>
> Are these ET people hostile? Well, if they were hostile, with their weaponry they could have destroyed us a long time ago or could have done some damage.

I know that some of the technologies came from the extraterrestrial craft. And, the reason they crashed is that their guidance mechanism was interrupted by our radar and by some equipment that we have.[5]

Fig. 10. Cattle mutilation sign.

We have learned from their technology; for example, we used other laser and plasma rays for our cattle mutilation experiments. Nobody ever says anything good about cattle mutilations, but we saved a lot of lives in Vietnam with this extraterrestrial technology for blood transfusion. That does not mean, however, that they are at war with us.

We have worked with the ET representatives through the 1954 Greada Treaty. Being able to communicate with them, we now know of at least four other extraterrestrial races with whom we have been in contact. According to Commander Graham Bethune (of the Disclosure Project), the four races are the Pleiadians, the Orionites, the Lyrans and the Grays.

The extraterrestrials warned us not to do certain things—for instance, not to bring weapons to a meeting set up between them and us. Our security forces nevertheless carried weapons, and the ammunition exploded, starting a battle that ended in twenty-two extraterrestrial and about thirty-nine human deaths. We never understood exactly what made the ammunition explode, but they had warned us and we didn't listen. It was probably their personal force fields that set off the ammunition.

I will stand on this fact: I have never read in any government file or document within the intelligence agencies that an ET ever deliberately hurt a human being—not once. I can see only the good they have done and why they have come.

The main question the government has asked them is, "What did you come here to do?" Unfortunately, the government has its own plans for its citizens and the world, and this does not coincide with what the extraterrestrials want. That is why they will disclose their presence if the government attempts to continue the veil of secrecy.

✳ ✳ ✳

The great teachers—Buddha, Mohammed, Christ, White Buffalo Calf Woman, Quan Yin and more—have spoken about unconditional love. This is what the Christ consciousness is about. After his crucifixion, Christ came back in a new body in another dimension. It is my belief, through reading the New Testament, that he had really particlized to the seventh through ninth dimension.

Theosophy teaches that each dimension has about nine octaves to advance through. For how long? Forever, until you become pure light or energy or beyond, as Elizabeth Klarer speaks of. You become pure "God-ness," then you create your own world, your own star. The Native American and African cultures have symbols that represent the cosmos and our cosmic family. A grandfather or grandmother would show a child the night sky and point out the stars. A being of cosmic origin can become one with those stars.

Klarer says in *Beyond the Light Barrier*:

> The knowledge of the Universe has always existed. Even the Greeks knew of the unified field within the electromagnetic wavelength of light which comprises all of creation, bringing it into their alphabet. Alpha, Beta, Gamma, Delta—a harmonic sound to interact the four forces of light, the rhythm resonating within our brains to give us the alpha rhythm of achievement, where equanimity maintains a part of everyday life, as long as no conflict is involved.

A simple equation gives us the answer to the unified field propulsion systems for interstellar spaceships. A unified field equation of seven-figure harmonics is the key to space travel.

Universal harmonics is the mathematics used by Akon's civilisation. He speaks of harmonic maths, an harmonic affinity with all substance, a resonance tuned to matter itself expressed in terms of light.

This simple equation is clearly in my mind. The harmonic of anti-gravity through the harmonic of light being doubled, alters the geometric of time, and our awareness of reality in the physical sense will shift from one spatial point to another. This is based on space-time geometrics within the unified field which permeates all of existence.

Of all the many thousands of Earth scientists, only Einstein could find the simplicity of the Universe in his harmonic equation $E=mc^2$ . . . and look what came out of it—the atomic bomb, the destruction of material substance, or conversion into pure energy. He achieved this by maintaining a fairly continuous alpha rhythm in brain patterns of relaxed attention.

Akon, as a great scientist (physicist) can reverse the process; physical substance in any desired shape is produced from pure energy. Hence, the atomic structure of the interstellar spaceships of light, completely smooth and all in one piece. The composition of the material of the spaceship is conducive to energizing to generate the unified field propulsion systems. As a natural celestial object, she achieves a shift in space and time, in the frequency of light, so very different to the 'nuts and bolts' flying saucers constructed by men of Earth, which are purely atmospheric craft and propelled by jets.

Akon's spaceship resonates at harmonics tuned to light between the two cycles of matter and anti-matter manifesting in alternate pulses, moving instantaneously therefore, through the double cycle, within the electromagnetic wave-length of the Universe, and using the fabric of space itself by altering the space-time geometric matrix. The spaceship herself acts as a protection for the people within her, as she changes position through the unified field.

We are all creatures of light, composed of microatoms, the ultimate particle, built up from a combination of wave-lengths of the creative force, which we call light—or God.[6]

If we can shift *consciously*, it will not affect those who remain in the third dimension. We need to decide to enter cosmic consciousness. That is truly what life with a Cosmos clearance is about—beyond the military, beyond the government, beyond ourselves and into the Fifth World.

Notes

1. Elizabeth Klarer, *Beyond the Light Barrier* (Aylesbury, UK: Howard Timmins Publishers, 1980).
2. Ibid.
3. Ibid., 49–50.
4. Jim Wilson, "America's Nuclear Flying Saucer," *Popular Mechanics* (November 2000).
5. Steven M. Greer, M.D., *Disclosure: Military and Government Witnesses Reveal the Greatest Secrets in Modern History* (Crozet, Va: Crossing Point, Inc., 2001), 379.
6. Klarer, *Beyond the Light Barrier,* 189-190.

CHAPTER FOUR

FROM VOID TO MASS:
WAVE PARTICLIZATION

I n 1949, I was in charge of the military's climatic testing at the Eglin Air Force Proving Ground in Florida. This is where the government had the largest climatic hangar in the world at the time. They could test anything in temperatures between 220 degrees above and below zero Fahrenheit. I worked then under Benoit Mandelbrot. This was when I was introduced to the concept of particlization and before my field of investigation became UFOs and extraterrestrials.

In subatomic physics, there are two states or realities: particles and waves. A wave can be understood as a state of motion, a nonphysical reality not limited by this or any other universe. Everything that enters our universe comes in as a wave—light, sound, even emanations from the Sun. If you want to change a wavelength (the characteristic of a wave), which is pure light and energy, into mass, then you convert it to particles. The military calls this particlization. Particlization is the principle behind time travel.[1]

The famous Philadelphia Experiment in 1943 resulted in the teleportation—and, as it turned out, the time travel—of the USS Eldridge (a megaton destroyer) from its dry dock in the Philadelphia naval yard to Norfolk, Virginia, a distance of about four hundred miles. In that experiment, scientists had mistakenly cut the middle of a wavelength, changing the frequencies between dimensions and thereby knocking a hole in space-time. If you don't get the wave just right, the object disappears on some part of the wave and reappears on another and the molecules and particles are changed. The military was trying to make the ship radar-invisible, but as can often happen in experiments, there were unexpected results. Instead of the ship becoming invisible to radar, it moved to another location and altered time in a way that was not then understood. When the ship reappeared, its bulkhead had been interpenetrated by the bodies of many crewmen. We had changed both the time and space that the ship and its crew had occupied.

The wave field is infinite. It surrounds and interpenetrates everything. A blade of grass, a tree or a stone is really an entity with an unlimited consciousness. Although they do not move themselves, they receive waves. Even a rock has memory; it remembers that it has existed for millions of years, possibly in one spot. Indigenous peoples can read rocks; machines have also been created to help us do that. NASA learned how to read the history of rocks and spent a lot of time and effort analyzing the rocks brought back from the Moon. Bacteria are some of the life forms that allow us to read history and thereby project our future.

In fact, from documents I have seen, the National Security Agency (NSA) uses subliminal posthypnotic scripts, which are implanted posthypnotic suggestions and scripts using acoustically delivered and phonetically accelerated commands for intelligence and counterintelligence applications.[2] We do this within the NSA. This is advanced-engineering knowledge of acoustic wave science and is the supreme intelligence tool derived from our years of work concerning particlization. This science can be applied to benefit humanity or to spy on humanity; this technology is "Big Brother." We currently have satellites with millimeter-wave technology that can get inside not only your house but your mind! This new research is called DNA scripting.

An entity is not necessarily physical; it can be an energy wave not limited to a specific universe or dimension. An entity is part of the All. There are both particle-based entities and non-particle-based entities. Wave entities can have intelligence and personality. Most of the time they are aware of who they are and where they are.

If you believe in some kind of supreme being or universal mind, then the knowledge contained within that cosmic consciousness can be accessed through all creatures. What the supreme being knows, its creatures know. The unique aspect of our human physicality is that our cells are archives for everything that ever was or is within the universe. Our cells contain that encoded history within our DNA. We are made up of everything that has been before, everything that is and everything that will be.

Particlization has been done not only by machines, but by the human mind and brain. It is possible to simply think something into existence, to actually form your own physical reality. Everything that comes into this system is in the form of a wavelength. A radio can be tuned to a specific frequency. Humans can also learn to do this; by picturing the reality one wants with an unobstructed focus, wave energy will assume that physical structure. This can be done with a radio, a car, even a rock or an egg.

Humans have the capability of transforming waves to particles because we have a pineal system. By organizing particles, humans can "create" (actually organize the energy of waves) and manipulate mass. Thus, human thoughts literally create human reality through the pineal gland. That is what makes human beings on Earth so unique among planetary species. The pineal gland (often called the third eye) not only has the ability to convert waves into particles and vice versa, it also allows us to travel in time and space. These particle patterns we create—signals, pictures, sounds, shapes and structures—resonate with our holographic belief systems. This is the science behind meditation, where mind, body and spirit come together.

We are apparently one of the few species with a gland that makes this possible. The extraterrestrials we have examined do not have a pineal system, but they are completely telepathic; however, we have not had enough to examine to determine whether other extraterrestrials might also have this system. But we know that many do not, which is one of the reasons they come here to study our development.

The Aborigines and the Dogon tribe claim their descendancy from Sirius. The Aborigines' traditional belief is that their Sirian ancestors decided to particlize and make themselves physical beings on Earth; they became whales and dolphins. It is possible for any being to experience physical reality on this planet. Species that are becoming extinct are actually moving into another dimension and will be in another school, another experience. Nothing is ever lost; all entities go on and on and on. New species come in as others go extinct. Sometimes a new species is an old species in a new form; sometimes a species might even dematerialize, which is essentially space-time travel.

The human brain is similar to a computer that perceives, views and creates mass. Our brain creates configurations of electrons that resonate with the worldview created by our subconscious beliefs. We can create a hologram, a picture that seems real in a waking state or a dream state. Have you sometimes dreamed and known it was real? It wasn't real in your waking reality, even though it seemed so. Sometimes you are traveling back in time or forward into the future. That may actually be the only place you can communicate with extraterrestrials, other-dimensional beings or any such phenomena. Humans have the ability to see these beings in other realms or states of mind.

© by Scott Collins.

Fig. 11. "Saponi Universe" by Scott Collins. Particle movement breaking apart from the wave via the pineal gland of the human brain.

There are ways for humanity to work with the pineal gland. In the time of Lemuria, the protrusion in the center of the forehead was a result of the sustained development of a faculty of the human body that has gradually disappeared since Lemuria submerged and its people were dispersed throughout the world. It was commonplace for the Lemurian to close his two physical eyes and to stand still at any moment of his daily activities, focus his consciousness upon the center of his forehead and receive an impression that might have been translated into one of sight, smell, hearing, feeling or tasting. In fact, it was as common for the Lemurians to turn their concentrated attention suddenly to this organ for some impression as it is for us today to stop in our conversation or activities and concentrate our attention upon our hearing in order to hear some distant or faint sound, or concentrate our eyes upon something we wish to see clearly, or concentrate our sense of smell or feeling for a moment in order to analyze some impression.[3]

Mayan schools taught time travel. The ancient indigenous cultures of the Americas, Tibet and Australia all have an advanced understanding of the space-time continuum. We should not be surprised to learn, therefore, that the art of mental telepathy or the mental exchange of ideas and impressions at unlimited distances became a perfectly natural, commonplace and regular practice for the Lemurians. They recorded, in a casual manner, the reception of impressions from others who were hundreds of miles away. That this sixth sense originated with an organ equal to—or in some way connected to—the present small organ in our bodies known as the pineal gland is quite likely. And scientists have discovered that in many of the races in remote parts of the world, this organ is much larger than in those of the civilized world. However that may be, this sixth sense also allowed the Lemurians to sense things in the fourth dimension.[4] We will realize at once that the Lemurians must have attained an extraordinarily high degree of perfection, not only in knowledge but in the matter of living and cooperating with all of nature's "cosmic laws."

This knowledge has allowed indigenous peoples to continue their development in spite of the many attempts at their genocide. The Tibetans know how to particlize through meditation and have taught it since ancient times. They have opened this knowledge to others within the past two to three hundred years. Buddha believed that every twenty-five thousand years, the wheel of dharma is turned afresh to help humanity reach a deeper consciousness.

The last cycle ended in the sixth century, during Buddha's lifetime. The end of the next cycle is 2012, the same year the Mayan cycles end.

Fig. 12. "The Tibetan Dharma Wheel."

Physics tells us that our planet is constantly bombarded with waves, which means that all forms of life come here in this way. These forms are created by light that utilizes wavelengths in special reality and then materializes them. Forms come from other dimensions and then are seen by our eyes. Even structures can be materialized this way—perhaps the structures of Tiahuanaco or the pyramids of Egypt. Knowledge about how to move objects through space (teleportation) was brought here by extraterrestrials. In the UFO era, we often view dematerializations. Sometimes we see a UFO craft sitting in the sky, unmoving; then it disappears, only to reappear in another place or at a different time.

✱   ✱   ✱

As long as we think we are only a body, we are subject to death. When we realize that we are *not* a body, that the real self is a waveform, we have no limitations. That's what particlization is all about. In a waveform you can go to another dimension, another solar system or another galaxy. In that state you are one with the Universal Mind, or the universal "computer." It might take years, but you can eventually discover the truth about anything that exists anywhere.

Since the beginning of mankind, guideposts and secret organizations have existed that will hasten your learning about this universal computer. In the ancient past, you might have spent twenty-five thousand years trying to obtain the knowledge of your evolution. There were mystery schools in the past where you could learn these things, but this is no longer necessary. You need not search for a wise teacher; you *are* that teacher. The ability is inherent within you; you don't have to meditate on a mountain or find someone to teach you.

From a holographic perspective, an extraterrestrial is simply a dimensional experience of yourself and your reality. It is possible to become aware of yourself in other-dimensional experiences during your dreamtime or even in the waking state. When your consciousness enters the dream state, you can experience yourself in other realms, becoming aware in two dimensions at once. You might even have experienced being an ET on some other planet or universe in the past or even the future.

Every system has other dimensions within it—harmonics, Pythagoras called it. Pythagoras, a Greek teacher and philosopher in the sixth century B.C., made use of a theory of harmonics called the *monochord*. He believed the universe was formed by a universal consciousness through harmonics, or color. The mathematical relationship of intervals on a musical scale was the same as that of nature, he taught. Every musical tone contains harmonics or overtones, higher frequencies that arise from the basic note, appearing in mathematical ratios of octaves.

Today's approach comes through quantum physics. A quantum wave is a wave of probability. When a wave collapses, it means that it has served its purpose. Sometimes it just disappears or changes into particles. In a way, that is what happened during the Rainbow Project part of the Philadelphia Experiment. The U.S. was successful when this was tried again during the Phoenix Project—also called the Montauk Project—in 1988 on Long Island.

By using magnetics and electricity, the government has also created a gravity-free lenticular reentry vehicle that separates gravity from space. This can be done with anything that spins, such as a gyroscope, whose spin harnesses the force of gravity. Most UFOs use this principle to power themselves by having a circular shape whose outer edge rotates. These can be considered the Model-T of UFOs. On the other hand, motherships, cigar-shaped craft, need only a small electromagnetic propulsion system. These more advanced craft are used for interplanetary travel where warp speed is needed. (Warp 4 would be four times the speed of light.) The military knows of about seventeen or eighteen different types of extraterrestrial spacecraft that vary in shape, mass and propulsion system.

✳   ✳   ✳

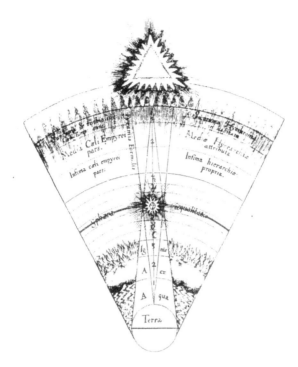

Fig. 13. Consonances of the monochord: The mundane monochord consists of a hypo-
thetical string stretched from the base of the pyramid of energy to the
base of the pyramid of substance.[5]

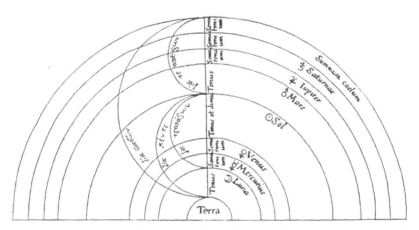

Fig. 14. The intervals and harmonics of the spheres: In the Pythagorean concept of
the music of the spheres, the interval between the Earth and the sphere of the six
stars was considered to be a diapason, the most perfect harmonic interval.[6]

We have to know before 2012 where our planet is heading; the year 2012 is the end of the 26,000-year Mayan cycle as revealed in one of their calendars. Carlos Barrios of the Organization for Mayan and Indigenous Spiritual Studies is an expert on the Mayan calendar. According to him, the world will not end in 2012. He says that the Mayan calendar, the Tzolk'in, was devised ages ago and was based on the cycles of the Pleiades. As he explains, when the right arm of the materialistic world is disappearing slowly but inexorably, then we are at the cusp of the era when peace begins and people live in harmony with Mother Earth. We are no longer in the world of the Fourth Sun, but we are not yet in the world of the Fifth Sun. This is the in-between time, the time of transition. As we pass through this transition, there is a colossal global convergence of environmental destruction, social chaos, war and ongoing earth changes.[7]

According to Barrios, the Mayan day keepers view the December 21, 2012, date as the rebirth, the start of the world of the Fifth Sun. It will be the start of a new era resulting from and signified by the solar meridian crossing the galactic equator and the Earth aligning itself with the galaxy. At sunrise on December 21, 2012, for the first time in 26,000 years, the Sun rises to conjunct the intersection of the Milky Way and the plane of the ecliptic. The Cosmic Cross is considered to be an embodiment of the sacred tree, the Tree of Life, a tree remembered in all the world's spiritual traditions.[8]

As spiritual beings we must develop our space-time ability and direct our evolution. No godhead or extraterrestrial race can save us from ourselves. We must do it from within. The universe does not circle around our planet; we are expanding into infinity. As human beings we are now breaking through. We must realize that we can use thought to particlize a wave into physical reality, a wave whose potential contains our vision. We can realize this knowledge through our practice of consciously combining body, mind and spirit through meditation, prayer, mantras, chants, Sun dance and the drum. It is all within the heart; if you want to know how to keep space, to keep time, put your hand on your heart as you go within.

The Hopis say that we have entered another world, another consciousness—the Fifth World. They say that the entire world will experience purification, and only the people of the Way of Peace will survive to usher in the New Age of the Sixth World.

We are in a great transition, the beginning of a new consciousness; some of us are already in the fourth dimension going toward the fifth. We are seeing into the future as well as the past, allowing us to become who we really are. It is our responsibility to pass this on, carrying a message that can lift the hearts of humanity.

Notes

1. For more information on particlization, see Stephen W. Hawking, *A Brief History of Time: From the Big Bang to Black Holes* (New York: Bantam Books, 1988).
2. For a complete document on the NSA's subliminal posthypnotic scripts, go to http://psychicspy.com/nsa-psy.txt.
3. Wishar S. Cervé, *Lemuria: The Lost Continent of the Pacific*, vol. XII (San Jose: Rosicrucian Press, 1931).
4. Ibid.
5. Manly P. Hall, *The Secret Teachings of All Ages: An Encyclopedic Outline of Masonic, Hermetic, Qabbalistic and Rosicrucian Symbolical Philosophy* (Los Angeles: Philosophical Research Society, 1928), lxxxi.
6. Ibid.
7. www.sacredroad.org.
8. Ibid.

CHAPTER FIVE

VIENNA AND THE BLACK SUN

T he symbols from the ancient worlds of Babylonia, Assyria, Egypt and
Phoenicia have been used by secret societies for thousands of years,
right into today's world.[1] When Adolf Hitler became associated with
the two major secret brotherhoods in Vienna—the Thule Society and the Vril
Society—he was plunged into a world of esoteric symbols and concepts. They
ultimately became the doctrines that led to the formation of the Third Reich.

The Black Sun, for example, symbolized the polarized energies emanating
from the center of the galaxy and thus the influence behind the movement
from the astrological Age of Pisces to the Age of Aquarius. This cyclic change
was felt not only in Germany,
but everywhere. In the Christian
Church, the faithful prepared for
the Second Coming of Christ.
But Hitler believed that the
Antichrist would usher in that
change and felt he had been
chosen to lead the world. If there
were to be a revolution, a New
World Order, he would be its
forerunner; in his mind, he was

Fig. 15. The Black Sun.

the Antichrist, and he declared as much in *Mein Kampf*, which he wrote in prison.[2]

Through these two secret societies, ancient Sumerian texts were being transcribed through telepathic communications from the Aldebaran System, which had a major influence on them. The symbol for the Vril Society, adopted later by the SS, is a dark circle surrounding two *sigs*, letters from the Germanic rune alphabet representing "*Sieg*" (victory). The Black Sun with a dagger piercing the center became a symbol of the Third Reich itself. This symbol came to rule heart, soul and spirit in darkness. Its wearer was personally committed to Hitler—not to the Third Reich or Germany, but to Hitler himself. Thus Hitler became the people's godhead through the initiation of the blood flag ritual. (The Nazi flag, red with a black swastika on a white circle, was called the blood flag.)

Fig. 16. Sig rune on a UFO.

According to reports I have seen from the UK's spy network (MI-5, MI-6), the French underground and the U.S.'s Office of Strategic Services (OSS), these two secret societies were communicating with distant worlds in 1917 Vienna.[3] Two female spirit mediums were guiding these occult lodges: the medium Maria Altish and a woman named Sigrun. Many occult lodges were rising in Europe at that time: the Illuminati, the Knights of Malta, the Knights Templar, the Freemasons, the Neo-Templars, the Rosicrucians (the Rose Cross), the Theosophists and the Black Sun organization. They all had studied the prophecies about a "New Babylon."

These secret societies were rejuvenated after the Crusades, but they were going in different directions. Yet they all saw the approach of the "new age." They held large parades in Vienna and major cities in Germany, where each group had its own temples and rituals for the coming age. They adopted Hitler as the commander of the New World Order because he empowered them. Hitler adopted the Thule Society; it not only studied the black arts, as did the Vril Lodge, but claimed contact with races beyond this planet. Hitler's main interest was in the communications about a new technology and the telepathic contact with this advanced race. This supported his goals for an Aryan super-race and its associated eugenics campaign.

Fig. 17. A Masonic apron with skull and crossbones.[4]

In 1919, the Thule Society was centered in Munich, and in 1921, one of its meetings was attended by Dr. Winfried Otto Schumann, a leading physicist in the field of alternative energy. Maria Altish, the spirit medium, had been receiving an ancient Sumerian alphabet, which became the secret code of the Knights Templar. The Templars had brought back many secret doctrines and prophecies after the Crusades, as did many other occult orders. Altish brought forward these ideas, which Hitler seized as necessary to the New World Order. He gave chosen secret societies the power to flourish, but he had his own agenda.

Sigrun was a trance medium who received technical formulas for an advanced technology. She communicated with beings from the Aldebaran System, which contains the brightest stars in the constellation of Taurus. She eventually allied herself with the Vril Society, offering this technology (and investments in it) to the industrial complex in partnership with Dr. Schumann, who was looking for an energy source for a new technology that would make space travel practical. The goal was to free Germany from dependence on fossil fuels in order to reach the stars.

Both good and evil are a creation of the universe—light and dark, positive and negative, yin (a discharging force field) and yang (a charging force field). The Black Sun is simply a symbol for the dark taken from the ancient past. This period in Europe saw a battle of the polarities of light and dark, black and white, occult and open wisdom. Hitler led the way into darkness. He was a fanatical believer in the power of the black arts and a studious reader of every text on occult practices. The secret societies could have chosen any leader, but Hitler struck a keynote for them with their mutual beliefs, symbols and rituals. He often said that power without religion would go nowhere. He needed a religion to mount his campaign on and unify the esoteric orders, and they expected a leader. So he convinced them that he was the one they were expecting.

As Hitler forged ahead with his vision of the new age, he was determined to sacrifice anyone he had to. He would ultimately eliminate those he believed did not belong in his new world. One either had to follow him or be sacrificed. He saw this time as a great renewal, through destruction, that would create the new age. Hitler saw that dark and light existed side by side. He had actually set out to destroy what he believed was the dark side—the imperfect human—only to embody that himself.

Technology became the means to achieve the New World Order. One of the first projects of the new technology was to create a time machine. Hitler was guided here by Maria Altish and Sigrun. It was mainly the Vril Society that succeeded in its experiments with a time machine. By 1924, the experimental machine had been constructed in Abensberg, Germany, at the Messerschmitt factory. The ultimate goal was to visit other planets and races. Once quantum physics and particlization were understood, this could be done.

Fig. 18. Three German RFCs.

In the early 1920s, Germany was beginning to experiment with mind control and teleportation. Hitler had a purpose for his time machine, and he would come to depend on the Vril Society to obtain the secrets of the new technology. Although the technology could allow time travel either to the future or the past, Hitler wanted to go backward, because he wanted to prove that the Aryans were descendants of the ancient Babylonians. The Babylonians, he believed, were descendants of the Atlanteans, who had migrated to Earth from another planetary system.

In the 1930s, Hitler sent explorations to Tibet, South America and Egypt. In Tibet scientists measured the people's physical characteristics, because Hitler believed they were the closest living bloodline to the historical Babylonians. He also believed that the Aryans descended from the same bloodline. Every feature of the Tibetan physiology was carefully measured. The skull-measurement studies of Germans and Tibetans were published in Germany in the mid-1930s.

SS officers were to be the leaders of the new society. These typical German military men were to lead the Third Reich into the Aquarian Age, so SS men were encouraged to father many children. Hitler took all the people who fit the Aryan profile from countries throughout Europe and put them in his *Lebensborn* eugenics program. *Lebensborn* means "fountain of life"; it was a campaign for breeding babies. Thousands were bred in baby factories, with no parents. Hitler instructed young girls to become mothers; they would receive medals for the babies they birthed. He wanted to breed a new race of pure Aryan descent by concentrating the bloodline of the ancient Babylonians, a race ultimately from another world. This race would rule a thousand years.

Hitler believed that the Tibetans had a higher spiritual development than any other race on this planet. He knew that they could time travel, and he wanted that knowledge. He well understood that he must push forward with his master race plan so that he could become the Antichrist and usher in a golden age. He changed civilization through advanced war technologies, but this was never approved by the higher sources—what we call extraterrestrials. His reign did not end through peace and prayers or fasting, as with Gandhi or Nelson Mandela or Chief Joseph. It ended in the devastation wrought by bombs, warfare and genocide.

To this day, the secret philosophy of the Third Reich is veiled. Hitler appointed Heinrich Himmler, an expert geneticist, as Reichsführer of the SS, which expanded under his leadership. The SS was considered the elite of the master race, using the Black Sun and the twin sig runes as its symbol. There was also a Waffen-SS, a separate group used for organizing other countries. Himmler also established a spy ring as the security forces of the ruling SS. It used a skull and bones as its symbol and oversaw the death camps. The SS was meant to be the legacy of the Black Sun, the beam of energy from the galactic center that directly entered the heart to become either negative or positive.

The highest ranks of the National Socialist Party did not embrace these occult doctrines, so these groups had to take a back seat in party politics. They changed some of their writings to fit the political climate. However, Hitler supported their religions (at first) and convinced the political organizations that he was what they were looking for—their new messiah.

✳   ✳   ✳

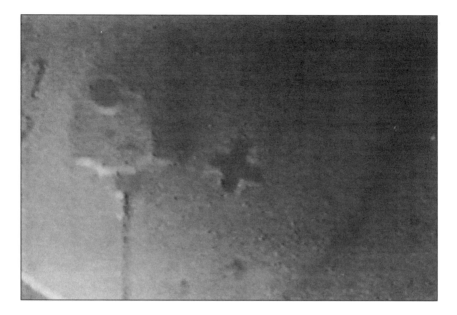

Fig. 19. The underside of a German Reproduction Vehicle with the Iron Cross and a laser weapon.

The German Iron Cross is another ancient symbol predating Christianity. The godhead of the cosmic inner light was in the form of a cross and represented the prophecy of the "New Babylon." In Babylonian times, the Maltese cross inside a circle was used by priests. This symbol has even been seen on photos of UFOs. Eventually it moved into modern times, such as in certain units of the CIA. This star and cross became the Star of David, two interlocking pyramids: one on Earth, the other pointing from heaven to Earth.

In esoteric symbology, the male body with its phallus has six extensions and is represented by the six-pointed star. This was adopted by Judaism in the belief that it is the seal of Solomon. The Knights Templar used the Star of David in their ceremonies and rituals. Of course, you can find the pyramid form throughout the world—in Central and South America, in the Far East and in Africa. Indigenous peoples used this symbol and some say the inverted triangle represents a triangular extraterrestrial vehicle (ETV) merging with the Earth to recharge, using the energy of Earth's grid lines as a power source.

Fig. 20. The occult doctrine of the Star of David with the
female vulva and birth of man and beast.[5]

As the Third Reich gained power, so did the science behind the Vril levitation machine and electromagnetic propulsion systems. Through the Thule and Vril Societies' trance communications, detailed information was obtained to manufacture these new propulsion systems. The Aldebaran System, where the information originated, is 68 light-years distant; Germany's technology was enabled to advance 250 to 450 years ahead of the technology of any other nation on Earth. Because Germany had the greatest scientific minds on Earth in the 1930s, perhaps it was logical for an extraterrestrial race to communicate with them. The technology could, after all, be developed there, inasmuch as one person, Hitler, had that kind of power.

In Germany at that time, quantum physics developed further than in any other nation. The U.S. had no spy network and thus had no idea what Germany was doing. It had a few great minds, such as T. Townsend Brown and Nikola Tesla, both known for their practical ability to direct theoretical physics through gravity and magnetics. But the Germans were far superior in their experiments and practical use of zero-gravity systems. Nobody in America was interested in this type of experiment until the 1940s.

When Dr. Schumann began attending meetings of the Thule and Vril Societies, his knowledge of alternative energy propelled the research on antigravity systems. Schumann developed and built the first large capacitor, which was used to stop the flow of electricity and store it, to be used later to accelerate German Reproduction Vehicles into space. It could store a million watts of energy.

In 1934, Hitler met with fellow Austrian Victor Schauberger. Schauberger was Germany's greatest quantum physicist in terms of anti-gravity propulsion systems. He told Hitler that his war machine, rockets and nuclear energy were based on false assumptions and that zero-gravity energy needed no fossil fuels or nuclear energy and would free Germany from its dependence on other nations. Schauberger was instructed to give a lecture to the Reichschancellors, because Hitler was interested in this new energy source.

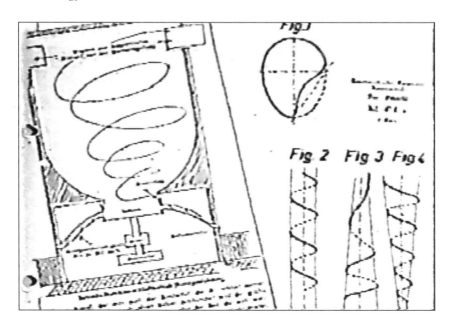

Fig. 21. Implosion diagram by Victor Schauberger.

Thus Schauberger was involved with the esoteric principles and the search for zero-gravity systems. He used Pythagoras's theories of the monochord, understanding that sound harmonics are the building blocks of the universe. By mathematically replicating the laws of nature, he utilized the alpha and omega wavelengths to mirror the components of spirit and matter. He ultimately developed a new science based on implosion, as opposed to explosion.[6]

The current energy sources—nuclear and fossil fuels—and the use of the internal combustion engine are destroying the environment and harming all life. They are based on a violent expansion of energy—explosion—whereas the implosion principle does not harm or pollute the environment; it is the formula for utilizing the free energy that surrounds us. Implosion occurs when an atom is caused to collapse or compress violently, similar to the collapse of a star, which becomes either a dwarf or a tiny black hole. Victor Schauberger lived for a time in Taos, New Mexico, where he shared ideas of nature with members of Taos Pueblo. He secretly worked at Los Alamos, but to his great disappointment, the implosion science he developed there was utilized for nuclear weapons.[7]

This advanced technology did not come about in a normal progression. We in the military who have Cosmos clearance know about extraterrestrial technologies and how we advanced in this area. Germany got this technology from outside this planet and so did the United States.

※　　　　　　※　　　　　　※

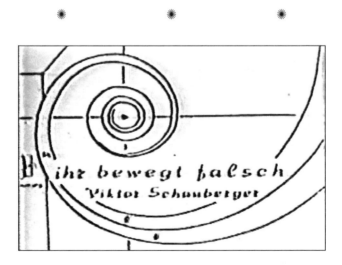

Fig. 22. Implosion diagram [vortex, seen from above] by Victor Schauberger.

Rudolph Hess was never freed; neither the Russians, nor the British or the U.S. wanted him free. He was heavily involved with the secret societies and was their main spokesman. He knew more about the secret societies, advanced technologies and extraterrestrial contacts than even Hitler. He was never pardoned because nobody wanted the ET presence and the secret technologies disclosed. In Hitler's Germany, Hess became the deputy Reichschancellor, but his interest remained with the doctrines of the occult lodges and the highly advanced propulsion systems. As Hitler moved forward with his master-race agenda, conquering the world for the Third Reich, Hess was attending the secret Thule meetings and listening to communications from Aldebaran, even conducting many of the society's meetings. The Thule Society covertly seated itself behind the Black Sun SS organization in manifesto. Hess was the number-two man in Germany, but he was really the number-one man in terms of being privy to secret technologies. Hess eventually saw that Hitler was going the wrong way with his war machine and eugenics campaign. He believed that the components of this advanced knowledge were spirit and matter, but he was a captive audience for the darkness of the Black Sun and followed Hitler's path. Hess went through the Nuremberg trials and was convicted. The allies did not want what he knew to be released or revealed.

Wernher von Braun was the scientist in charge of the new technologies the U.S. imported from Germany under the secret "Project Paperclip." At this time, our government is trying to convince our allies that we should weaponize space against terrorism. Information will ultimately be released to explain the real reason behind this—an extraterrestrial threat. The Black Sun and the secret doctrines behind it did not die with Hitler. It is present now in the destructive use of energy to build a New World Order. The result will be the destruction of our planet and all life upon it.

Within all space is tremendous power, far greater than what any internal combustion engine or nuclear power plant can create. If we could harness that energy, it would be the greatest source of free energy in the world; it couldn't be taxed because it is free. It burns nothing and never wears out because it has no moving parts. It can free the world, and at this moment the voices of humanity are crying out against the environmental effects of our energy systems, especially in Germany and France, because some know we have zero-gravity technology. They thought the U.S. would move forward with these new propulsion systems, but it has not. Instead, our current government wants to drill, to expand the use of fossil fuels and build many more nuclear power plants.

Hopi prophecy calls World War II the "Second Great Shaking" (they say the "Third Great Shaking" is the possible World War III). The U.S. (the "Great Babylon") is now the world's major military power and is marching toward complete domination of the planet. It leads the way in space exploration, back-engineered extraterrestrial technology and weapon building—all to build nests high in the heavens. As I understand it, the plan is to depopulate the planet.[8]

✳   ✳   ✳

The missile defense system is our government's last trump. Von Braun already pointed out that the U.S. will first blame Russia for the Star Wars program and then terrorism. Well, we have already parked nuclear weapons in space, but the trump card is the ET threat, meaning that we will be told that the extraterrestrials are sending weapons our way. Von Braun said that the last enemy to be sprung on humanity will be ETs in space.

Well, extraterrestrials can neutralize any weapon we have; they can even reverse nuclear energy. There is really no defense we can come up with now except the heart and spirit to counterattack the agenda of the Black Sun organization. Soon we will be told, "Guess what, we have found that other beings out there are far ahead of us, and we need to put these missile defense systems in place to counterattack," a scenario just like the invasion in *Independence Day,* which would justify these actions. This trump card they expect to play is a lie. The ETs have shut down our missile bases and nuclear reactors. This is what the Disclosure Project is telling people—that not only can the extraterrestrials do this, but they have done it already. They are so far advanced that if they wanted to destroy us, we wouldn't be here now. The military personnel testifying to this for the Disclosure Project have seen the proofs. The fact is, we can't destroy them, but they can neutralize anything and everything the militarists try to do.

The military-industrial complex is like the tentacles of an octopus and much more far-reaching than we can imagine. We are talking about a worldwide secret organization that continues the concept of a New World Order.

Most military people ignored what was happening in Germany, whereas the companies that made up our military-industrial complex were transacting business with the Third Reich. Many secret societies believed that Hitler would bring order to Europe and reveal the secrets of free energy. This period was the beginning of the cartel—the global web of financial interests—although the protocols for its establishment were outlined by the Bavarians in the 1700s. Cartels have become the greatest power since the beginning of history; these merchants sell Mother Earth to gain power and profit. Millions of dollars were transferred from the U.S. to Germany before WWII, building the Third Reich into an almost invincible power. "Babylon the Great" (the U.S.) and the Merchants of Mammon (wealth) everywhere are the economic elite. They are fueled by greed and have gathered colossal reservoirs of wealth.

However, the truth is coming to light, as with the Disclosure Project. Now it is up to us. I urge you to write to your Congresspeople, Senators and White House officials. Humanity has been cut out of the loop for too long. Eisenhower warned us to beware of the military-industrial complex, which cannot exist without war. The false threat of malevolent ETs is the next card to be played. Instead, they have always tried to help us and protect us from ourselves.

Wake up, America! You are your brother's keeper. Get interested, get educated. In the prophecies of Revelation, the United Nations (the "Temple of Babel") is helping to create the Great Tribulation, the final holocaust—a plan for the world by the international banking elite. The Antichrist power is the One World Government and its war machine, which is instigating World War III; the sign of the "Beast" is 666 and is the Merchants of War (the New World Order); "Babylon" is the United States. The Beast arises in the New World Order through the United States. The International Merchants and Bankers of Babylon are the international banking cartel, the New World Order or the One World Government of world finance, a worldwide web of combined interests. Its headquarters is the Great City Babylon—New York City, home of the United Nations. Players in the background are the Council on Foreign Relations, the Royal Institute of International Affairs, the Roundtable Groups, the Trilateral Commission, the Bilderbergs, the Illuminati, the Freemasons and the Order of Skull and Bones.[9]

Notes

1. See Eliphas Lévi, *Transcendental Magic*, trans. Arthur Edward Waite (York Beach: Red Wheel/Weiser, 1968); idem, *The History of Magic*, trans. Arthur Edward Waite (London: Rider & Company, 1957); William Henry, *One Foot in Atlantis* (Anchorage: Earthpulse Press, 1998); David Icke, *Robot's Rebellion: The Story of the Spiritual Renaissance* (Bath, England: Gateway Books, 1994); idem, *The Biggest Secret: The Book That Will Change the World,* second edition (Ryde, Isle of Wight: Bridge of Love Publications, 1999); Jim Marrs, *Rule by Secrecy: The Hidden History That Connects the Trilateral Commission, the Freemasons, and the Great Pyramids* (New York: HarperCollins, 2000); Michael Baigent, Richard Leigh and Henry Lincoln, *Holy Blood, Holy Grail* (New York: Dell, 1983); *Dan Salter UFO File I*, produced by Daniel M. Salter, 120 min., 1995, videocassette, Red Star Productions; and *Shadow of the Templars*, produced by Henry Lincoln, 60 min., A&E Ancient Mysteries, 1979, videocassette.

2. See Charles Higham, *Trading with the Enemy: An Exposé of the Nazi-American Money Plot* (New York: Delacorte, 1983); Maurice Chatelain, *Our Ancestors Came from Space* (New York: Dell, 1978); Manly P. Hall, *Lost Keys of Freemasonry* (Los Angeles: Philosophical Research Society, 1976); Nesta Webster, *World Revolution: The Plot Against Civilization* (Sedona, Ariz.: Veritas Publishing, 1994); *Covenant of Iron Mountain*, a Dan Salter film, n.d., videocassette, Red Star Productions ; and Leonard Lewin, *Report from Iron Mountain on the Possibility and Desirability of Peace* (New York: Dial Press, 1962). This last work is a satire written by Leonard Lewin, hatched by Victor Navasky and staff at *Monocle*, a "political satire rag," and abetted by editor E.L. Doctorow at Dial Press/Simon & Schuster.

3. *The Thule Society*, from Daniel M. Salter Archives, 51 min., n.d., videocassette, Red Star Productions.

4. Manly P. Hall, *The Secret Teachings of All Ages: An Encyclopedic Outline of Masonic, Hermetic, Qabbalistic and Rosicrucian Symbolical Philosophy* (Los Angeles: Philosophical Research Society, 1928), ixxvii.

5. David Wood, *Genisis: The First Book of Revelations* (Kent, England: Baton Press, 1985), 138.

6. See the Daniel M. Salter Archives, Red Star Productions.

7. Ibid.

8. *Koyaanisqatsi*, produced and directed by Godfrey Reggio, 87 min., Institute for Regional Education, 1982, film.

9. Marrs, *Rule by Secrecy,* 22–113.

CHAPTER SIX

GERMANY'S ADVANCED TECHNOLOGIES PRIOR TO AND DURING WWII

T he first modern government group involved in manufacturing advanced technology based on zero-gravity propulsion systems was the Nazi SS. They back-engineered two ancient extraterrestrial vehicles they had retrieved from the upper Amazon jungles of Brazil. To my knowledge—from military intelligence reports—these were the first such recovered extraterrestrial vehicles.

In World War I, Germany sent many privately financed expeditions to the far reaches of the globe, primarily led by Edmund Kist and Professor Sven Hedin. The secret agenda was to trace the migrations of an advanced Atlantean race in South America, Tibet and Egypt. They were looking for extraterrestrial technology that might have escaped the destruction of Atlantis. In the 1930s, Hitler went to great lengths to support his claim for Aryan descent, and when an indigenous tribal leader reported to the Brazilian government an ancient historical finding of an extraterrestrial spacecraft, an expedition was immediately sent.

In 1931 and 1932, a German team was led to the upper Amazon jungle and into underground chambers of an expansive tunneling system. They found two UFO craft at the entry.[1] After a financial arrangement was made with Brazil, the vehicles were transported by German submarine and delivered into the hands of the SS and the Vril Society. By 1935, the leading scientists of alternative-energy projects had back-engineered the UFO and had reproduced its antigravity propulsion system. The first experimental models were the Haunebu 1, 2, 3, 4 and 5. Later came the RFC-1, RFC-2, RFC-3, RFC-4, RFC-5, RFC-6 and RFC-7.

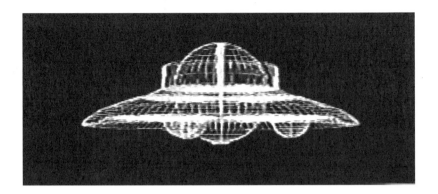

Fig. 23. Computer diagram of a Haunebu.

I also learned that thousands of *Ica* stones (gliptoliths, or engraved stones) were found in Brazil with inscriptions from the Ancient Ones. Dr. Javier Cabrera, who collected them, identified them as records of civilizations from off this planet.

✳   ✳   ✳

An Austrian scientist's discoveries and research were used by the Nazis to develop another new propulsion system that used the principle of implosion to neutralize gravity. Victor Schauberger, called the "water wizard," had been working on his own theories of tachometric propulsion in an attempt to understand what he had observed in natural water systems. Nature was his teacher, and water was the vehicle by which he created his new science. Through the principles applied in nature and the flow of water, Schauberger discovered systems making use of free energy based on the principle of levitation within water. In the living flow of energy of all natural waterways, Schauberger discovered the mysteries and patterns of the hyperbolic spiral. This vortex, or spiral, is formed from horizontal and vertical curves repeated in nature's patterns. It can be seen in the plant and animal kingdoms and even in our own bodies.

The spiral is an ancient symbol found throughout the world and revered by different cultures. It is used as the symbol of emergence from one world or state or dimension to another via dimensional doorways, something like a birth canal. All time, space, matter and spirit merge within the spiral.[2] All life moves between two polarities, and the hyperbolic spiral, or vortex, is formed between them. Within these movements or rhythms, energy is carried by centripetal and centrifugal forces. The centripetal or implosive force builds, moving toward the center, whereas the centrifugal or explosive force destroys, spiraling to the outside. These forces can be manipulated to create tachometric propulsion, the power of the vortex.

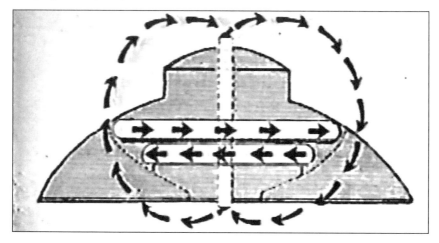

Fig. 24. Vril propulsion system (based on the principle of implosion).

The swastika in its positive and negative forms symbolizes these polarities, representing the duality of the natural forces. The German swastika is reversed, thus representing the negative use of these polarities. To Hitler it signified the victory of the Aryan race over inferior races. But the true swastika, the positive link, is also an ancient symbol for Atlantis, and in China it was inscribed on the Buddha for good luck. To this day, it is a religious emblem for Hindus. This symbol can be found too among the Hopi of the Southwest, where it symbolizes life and is given to boys when they are initiated into their religious practice.[3] Interestingly, the Nazi swastika symbol is also found in the field of radionics, where it represents the seventh chakra or the seventh ray, the healing ray.[4]

✳   ✳   ✳

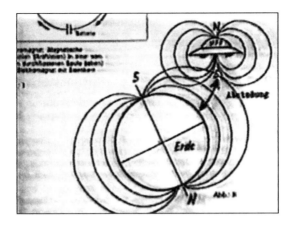

Fig. 25. Electromagnetic propulsion system diagram.

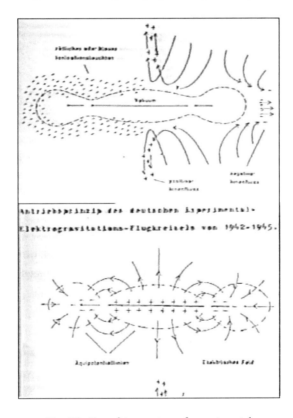

Fig. 26. Propulsion system of experimental
electrogravitational flying spintop (*Flugkreisel*).

Heinrich Himmler was an authority on metaphysics. Under him SS scientists experimented with extrasensory perception. They manipulated humans via radionics, beginning the first mind-control experiments that used human telepathic abilities as a biocosmic transducer. The induction of telepathic states was increased by the use of psychotropic drugs such as the Ayahuasca plant from Brazil. It is said that this plant allows a person to open the door to other dimensional worlds, that it allows a person to perceive through another person's senses and read his or her mind. These mind-control experiments ultimately allowed the SS to transmit messages telepathically.

The science of mind control was seized after World War II by intelligence groups such as the CIA and the National Security Agency (NSA), and they were called hypnotic scripts. The experiments conducted by the Nazis at Dachau using drugs and hypnosis ended up in America's backyard!

※　　　　　　　　※　　　　　　　　※

Germany had been involved with research on a time machine, which inspired a Vril levitation machine. SS-E4, a division of the SS, was involved in advanced projects like this. (I was always curious about the name S-4 at Area 51; it is the division that back-engineers the U.S.'s advanced extraterrestrial technology. Is such a close resemblance—SS-E4 and S-4—a coincidence?) With this new technology again came the physicist Dr. Winfried Otto Schumann, who was trying to find an energy source to replace oil. His expertise was in atomic physics and nuclear weapons, and he was well advanced in particlization. During World War II, the Allies bombed the heavy-water production facilities, where nuclear weapons were being manufactured using Dr. Schumann's research and death-camp slave labor.

The RFC-1 employed the principle of vortex energy. They had two models: one had a pancake shape with a dome in the center and the other was shaped like an egg. Hermann Göring, a principal military leader in the Third Reich, was determined that Germany would possess weapons and technology superior to that of any other nation on Earth. When he became a major investor in a German National Film Company movie project, that money ultimately helped finance Wernher von Braun's first space rocket. On von Braun's team was Herman Albert, who designed the first light aircraft, the Vril propulsion system, or RFC-2.[5] The Germans called it an *unbekanntes Flugobjekt*, an unidentified flying object.

This vehicle was about fifteen feet in diameter and was powered by magnetic impulse steering, free of gravity. It optically shifted when accelerating, so the faster it moved, the more it changed shape, and so did its lights—from violet to blue to red-orange to white. The SS-E4 went ahead with this research and continued to develop vessels based on the principles of ET vehicles. Had the National Socialist Party recognized the validity of this super-science and pursued its path more vigorously, Hitler might have won World War II. However, only the SS elite was interested in UFO technology.

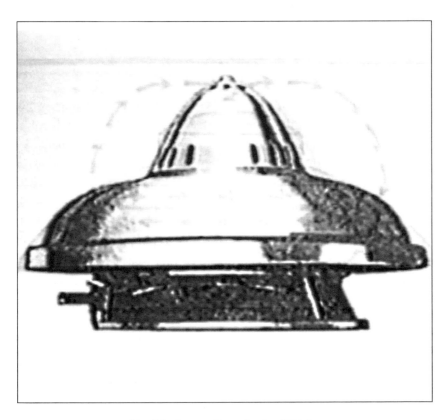

Fig. 27. German Reproduction Vehicle.

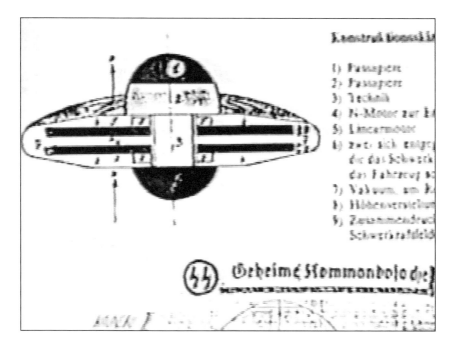

Fig. 28. German Reproduction Vehicle.

By 1938, there were three new jet-propulsion systems: the HE-138, HE-176 and HE-280. The SS also constructed a light aircraft, the RFC-4, using the Thule arrow engine. The purpose of this craft was to study how a disk-shaped object performed in flight. What really motivated the SS was the power of the negative use of solar energy, the "Black Sun"; as I said earlier, this Black Sun and the Nazi swastika became their symbols.

In 1939, Germany built the RFC-5, another antigravity machine. So we could say that by 1939, Germany had already built five successful Reproduction Vehicles. In the latter part of 1939 came the Haunebu 5, which was a larger and more complicated machine. It could carry up to four passengers and had separate storage compartments.

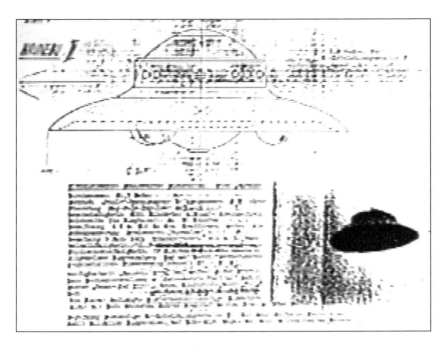

Fig. 29. Haunebu with zero-gravity propulsion system.

Fig. 30. German flying disk. Hitler viewing a model [foreground]
and a prototype [background].

In the Disclosure Project, Don Phillips testified that the U.S. now has these advanced technologies from which humanity could greatly benefit if the government dropped its secrecy. He testified that between the years 1950 and 1960, NATO did extensive studies into the origin of extraterrestrial races and forwarded this research to a number of foreign nations, including film footage of meetings with these ET races and high-ranking leaders of our own government.[6] Phillips was in the Air Force and worked under contract with the CIA at Lockheed Skunkworks on the design of the U-2 and the SR-71. Thus we got the technology from both Germany and the extraterrestrials.

✳   ✳   ✳

By 1939, the British spy network, MI-5 and MI-6, had learned that Germany possessed advanced technology. Soon after, General William "Wild Bill" Donovan organized the soldier spies of the Office of Strategic Services (OSS). In the military at that time, the feeling was that "gentlemen don't spy." That is what we used to say, and in the beginning we wouldn't listen to what the British intelligence said about Germany's advanced technologies. It was only when the U.S. had the hard facts that Germany was working on something "out of this world" that we figured we'd better stop being gentlemen and start spying. So America allied with the UK's spy network and we began our own—the OSS.

Our greatest field of advancement in the late 1930s and early 1940s was particlization, invisibility and teleportation. In the U.S. there were Dr. Nikola Tesla, Dr. John Hutchinson, Dr. Emil Kurtenauer, Albert Einstein and Dr. John von Neumann. Einstein postulated that time is another dimension and can be moved with electromagnetic fields into hyperspace. These experiments began in the thirties and by the forties had some success—the Philadelphia Experiment, the Montauk Project and the Rainbow Project.[7]

In 1939, Hitler invaded Poland, which was a great mistake and led to World War II. The many divisions of the German military—the Air Force, the Navy, the Army (and the war-production industries)—were following their individual ambitions. They did not unite to build secret weapons, so the new technology was not funded as well as the secret orders wanted. The military forces competed against one another for contracts: the Army wanted tanks and artillery, weapons such as the Cannon 88, which was the best; the Navy was building the world's best submarines; and the Army's Waffen SS got what it wanted. They eventually reached a compromise with the RFC-7, another Reproduction Vehicle. But this one had a pulse-beam weapon—the laser cannon.

Fig. 31. German Reproduction Vehicle with laser weapon.

Andreas Epp, another German zero-gravity engineer, designed a flying disk that was built in Breslau. This craft, called a "flying gyroscope," was engineered to fly on a transmitted beam directed by a code word; it had a successful test near Prague. The craft was large, with a central dome. It basically homed back to its base on the beam. We do this with our automatic direction finder (ADF). The energy of a spinning gyroscope is stable as long as the speed is constant.

By 1940, Germany had a small RFC-2, which was a reconnaissance vehicle, and the *Andromeda*, a mothership that could carry several Haunebus at one time. The RFC-2 was like a satellite, a spy machine that could collect data from other European nations. That was its job. In 1941 appeared an RFC-6 and a Haunebu 2, both of which were able to rendezvous and land upon the large supply ship *Atlantis*.

Fig. 32. The mothership *Andromeda*, a cigar-shaped German craft on which up to seven Haunebus could be loaded.

In 1940, Germany began its transport missions to the Antarctic. The world had divided the Antarctic in the late 1930s, and next to America and Argentina, Germany claimed more than anyone else—at least two hundred thousand square miles. The Germans named this territory *Neu-Schwabenland*. To my knowledge, the Third Reich started an underground complex there in about 1938, headed by Hermann Göring. The Germans disguised it as a scientific mission. The part of the Antarctic the Germans chose was not an ice shelf; it had tundra where grass grew when the ice melted and the land was exposed. Antarctica is not all ice, as most people think. In the territory they chose, the ice melted at certain times of the year, which enabled the Third Reich to build their underground city.

By the end of 1942, Germany had a jet-propelled vertical aircraft, the Schriever-Habermohl 262. It was a large cigar-shaped vehicle built in the old Zeppelin hangar in Germany. (The U.S. built one later and named it the *Zeppelin*.) Nobody knew that in 1942 the Germans had built the *Andromeda* mothership, which could travel to other planets and take along some Haunebus and what we called Foo fighters.

Dr. Richard Meter worked on a disk-shaped RFC-7 that was powered by Volkswagen and BMW turbine engines. The turbine engines did not adapt well to outer space where Earth's atmosphere ends. Internal combustion engines must have air, so the RFC-7 lost power in proportion to its altitude. Italy was involved in the engineering design for the new German technology; Giuseppe Belluzzo developed an experimental supersonic helicopter using unconventional energy. This vehicle, the V-7, could attain an altitude of approximately eighty thousand feet and had a zero-gravity propulsion system.

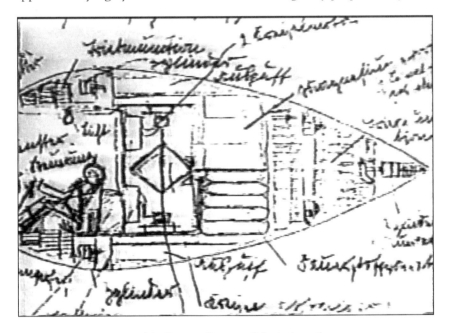

Fig. 33. German diagram of the *Andromeda*.

At the close of World War II in late 1945, Truman issued an executive order. Headed by Admiral Delmer S. Fahrney and the Naval War Committee, Truman authorized the collection of all of the Third Reich's UFO technology that could be obtained. This was a secret project called Paperclip and was when we imported the best German scientists, headed by Wernher von Braun. Then we began to employ the best people Germany had in the field of electromagnetic propulsion systems. This was really the beginning of the top-secret Cosmos unit. Project Paperclip was about rockets, but Cosmos was concerned with electromagnetic propulsion systems.

The first actual "space city" was built by Germany at Peenemünde. It was designed by Dietrich Eckhard and Rudolf von Sebottendorf. The British spy network found out about it and bombed Germany to stop rocket launches and destroy the different types of extraterrestrial vehicles that Germany had been back-engineering. The Germans had been studying and building space technologies that were not only capable of reaching space, but were in fact sustaining themselves there. They intended to place the first man on the Moon. Vehicles launched from Peenemünde also went to Mars and Venus.

At first the UK associated the German technology with some form of air balloon or similar advanced technology. However, they found that Peenemünde was launching the V-1 and V-2 rockets against London. The Germans used a crude gyro system to point and direct the rockets. This work was under the leadership of von Braun. They did not always know where the rocket would land, because it dropped whenever the fuel burned out. Sometimes a rocket would malfunction and destroy city blocks and historic landmarks like cathedrals. As a result, they built huge ramps and tried to develop an unmanned guidance system. However, they still needed pilots on their intercontinental rockets for accuracy, and some were women.

Eventually they improved their unmanned guidance systems with expulsion jets and improved their gyroscopes by shifting weight as the fuel burned. Germany tried to convince Britain that they had no chance against the German war machine. However, the U.S. had more military resources and, becoming an ally of the UK, produced more and better weapons to defeat the Axis powers.

✳   ✳   ✳

In the U.S. archives are speculations that Germany and Japan could have succeeded in a one-way mission to Mars before the close of World War II. It is suspected that Germany and Japan may have been successful in completing the Mars mission in a Haunebu 5. (In fact, the U.S., Russia and some German scientists manufactured a replica of the Haunebu 5, which successfully completed a mission to Mars.) Although Japan was not as technologically advanced as Germany, Germany needed Japan to finance its space technologies and Japan wanted the new technology.

Many people to this day don't know that both Germany and Japan secretly believed in the existence of a superior race that had been visiting Earth from time immemorial. The Japanese believed they were the descendants of the Sun gods, a super-race. Japan does not have the sunburst on its flag anymore; when the Japanese were defeated, they reverted to their earlier symbol of a red circle. If Japan and Germany had united sooner, between the sheer population numbers and the technology, we might not have been able to catch up. Also, if Germany had given Japan its new technology, Japan could easily have duplicated it, but Germany refused to hand it over. It wasn't until after Pearl Harbor that Japan and Germany united forces.

During World War II, when our bomber squadrons were flying over Germany, the pilots came in contact with what they called Foo fighters. Germans called them *Fliegende Schildkröten* ("flying turtles") and *Feuerkugeln* ("fire balls"). They were exactly that—balls of fire that could pace right off the wingtips. No maneuver could shake them off; they could even get in front of the windshield. Pilots couldn't lose them or fire at them. They were so fast, gunners would never get a chance.

Foo fighters were an unmanned flying ball of light that could make the gauges useless. They were electromagnetic and could kill the engines of a bomber squadron. The B-17s, our Flying Fortresses, would start to descend, and only when the bomber was far enough away from the Foo fighter could he regain control—if he didn't hit the ground first. Only in that dive could he reclaim his electrical system. The Foo fighters appeared as a light, but an actual vehicle was there. Sometimes a B-17 would collide with a Foo fighter, and in the wreckage an actual object would be found.

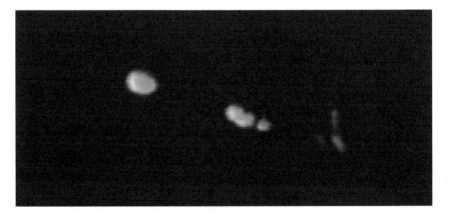

Fig. 34. Foo fighters.

In the air space over Germany, our pilots also saw disk-shaped UFO craft. Germany had manufactured laser weapons to mount on the underside of these disks. At the end of the war, we recovered some of these German craft. Texas Instruments, Inc. reengineered the weaponry, and that is where our pulse-beam weapons came from—German ET-based technology that utilized laser weaponry.

The New York Times

THURSDAY, DECEMBER 14, 1944

Floating Mystery Ball Is New Nazi Air Weapon

SUPREME HEADQUARTERS, Allied Expeditionary Force, Dec. 13—A new German weapon has made its appearance on the western air front, it was disclosed today.

Airmen of the American Air Force report that they are encountering silver colored spheres in the air over German territory. The spheres are encountered either singly or in clusters. Sometimes they are semi-translucent.

SUPREME HEADQUARTERS, Dec. 13 (Reuter)—The Germans have produced a "secret" weapon in keeping with the Christmas season.

The new device, apparantly an air defense weapon, resembles the huge glass balls that adorn Christmas trees.

There was no information available as to what holds them up like stars in the sky, what is in them, or what their purpose is supposed to be.[8]

The U.S. brought German scientists to America so that we could jump-start our own technology. The SS facilities were relocated to keep their space technology going. Even though Germany surrendered, the Third Reich itself never did. Hermann Göring was charged with moving what he could out of Europe to the Antarctic, Argentina and Brazil. The U.S. military knew that a hundred German submarines transferred people and technology systems out of Germany to these three locations, and we have never accounted for those missing people or equipment. The Haunebus, the Vrils and jet rockets were all transferred out of Germany. However, word has it in intelligence circles that we obtained approximately thirty advanced antigravity technology systems from the close of World War II, thereby enabling us to forge ahead with our own Reproduction Vehicles. At the same time, Russia also retrieved documents, files and possibly vehicles. We have no knowledge of exactly how much they got, but this certainly was the initial reason for the Star Wars program.

The Nazis may have made use of a vast ancient underground tunnel system in Antarctica. For thousands of years, there have been underground tunnel systems in Mesoamerica, Alaska and the Antarctic, long before these areas were invaded by the Germans or colonized by England or the United States. In 1947, Admiral Richard E. Byrd and Admiral Wood were sent on what was called Operation High Jump, with battleships and military aircraft. The purpose was to find the missing technology. The public was told that it was a military contingent for geological research. But after almost a year and major funding, the U.S. hit a dead end. The U.S. military also made expeditions to the Antarctic to investigate intelligence reports of UFO activity.

After everything that happened in Germany at the close of World War II, how many people know that we obtained extraterrestrial technologies from Germany? America's military still does not want people to know that the days of the internal combustion engine must soon be a thing of the past; they do not want a worldwide collapse of the fossil fuel industry. The secret of our progress has been kept under guard by the covert intelligence agencies—till now.

The less we abuse the Earth, the sooner she will heal. The blood of the Earth is her water, as Schauberger has said. We have polluted our rivers, then dammed them so they cannot heal themselves. Earth's blood doesn't flow like it used to, and we have torn holes in our heavens.[9] We need to start thinking about our Earth and help her recover as much as we can. Each race has a responsibility for an element in nature—earth, air, fire and water. The extraterrestrials contacted our government because they did not want war on Earth or in space.

The extraterrestrials were there; they look like us, and some of them live among us even now. They have been through a nuclear war and know it could happen to us. It's up to us. Time has speeded up, and there is not much left. Sometimes I think I've got the answers, but nobody asks me. We must decide within the next four or five years where we want to be in this planetary transformation. Wake up; we have a history that goes back thousands and millions of years. Life evolves in different forms, and we all have had many lives, not only on this planet but on many other planets.

We do not need extraterrestrials from outer space to save us, to correct us, to improve us. We need an alliance with inner space. Another law or regulation or a court decision will not do it. Only a profound change in us will do it. There are no committees for the soul.

Notes

1   See Karl Brugger, *The Chronicle of Akakor* (New York: Delacorte Press, 1977).

2. *Fractals: The Color of Infinity*, directed by Nigel Lesmoir-Gordon, 54 min., 1994, videocassette.

3. David Monongye (Hopi Elder), "Holding Fast to the Path of Peace: A Traditional View" (n.p., n.d.).

4. David V. Tansley, *Chakras: Rays and Radionics* (Woodstock, N.Y.: Beekman Publishers, Inc., 1984).

5. *The Thule Society*, from Daniel M. Salter Archives, 51 min., n.d., videocassette, Red Star Productions.

6. Steven M. Greer, M.D., *Disclosure: Military and Government Witnesses Reveal the Greatest Secrets in Modern History* (Crozet,Va.: Crossing Point, Inc., 2001), 375–383.

7. For more information, see Preston B. Nichols with Peter Moon, *The Montauk Project: Experiments in Time* (New York: Sky Books, 1992).

8. "Floating Mystery Ball Is New Nazi Air Weapon," *New York Times*, 14 December 1944, 10.

9. *Holes in Heaven*, directed by Wendy Robbins, 51 min., Gallina Projects and Paula Randol-Smith Productions, 1998, videocassette.

CHAPTER SEVEN

THE BROTHERHOOD LODGES

Hitler could never have come to power had he not been financially supported by key world leaders, who still orchestrate events. The Brotherhood of the Black Sun and its secret orders are supported by the highest level of scientific and technological genius, which includes esoteric occult knowledge, mind control, psychic powers, genetic engineering and quantum physics used in service to the black arts. Politically, their secret knowledge and technology are moving the world toward the New World Order, through which absolute control can be established and maintained. With regard to their fulfillment of this agenda, there also exists on this planet and in other universes a guiding force of the true White Brotherhood, who upholds cosmic law to benefit all of humanity.

The post-World War II Star Wars program has been led by the United States, Russia, China, Israel and the United Kingdom. Hundreds of German scientists and intelligence specialists were transferred to covert projects within secret departments in the governing infrastructures of the U.S., Russia, Brazil, Argentina and the UK to jump-start this program.

The organization of the Brotherhood and its global web can be seen through the initiatory organization of the secret societies. For example, in the Ancient and Mystical Order of the Rosicrucians (AMORC), when an initiate passes into the final degree, he moves on to the Illuminati and through further degrees passes into the Brothers of the Rose Cross. Then the initiate is on the level of the Grand Masters of the Priory of Sion, the deepest inner circle of the Templars ("Sion" stands for the Egyptian figures Set, Isis, Osiris and Nephthys).[1]

The ascending orders reflect the many levels of initiation rituals practiced

Fig. 35. The Rose Cross of the Rosicrucian Brotherhood. The Rose Cross developed from the *crux ansata*, which originated with the Egyptian mysteries.[2] This revival was sparked in the seventeenth century through Rosicrucianism.[3]

by these secret societies to consolidate power and ensure secrecy, all of which is underpinned by the knowledge handed down from the ancient mystery schools. These Brotherhood orders have chosen to use the negative polarity of that power. We can see today how modern secret societies have manipulated the original teachings for the purpose of personal power.

Modern Masons are called Freemasons; this branch began in America when George Washington and others urged their countrymen to free themselves from the old Masonic order in Europe. The Illuminati ("the enlightened ones," or "the angel-men") want a one-world government, not a government "for the people, by the people." This one-world alliance is rising up through the UN and NATO, which it uses to preemptively further its own agenda. This forward move is rapidly advancing today. We must decide whether to allow a one-world government under their control. If we do not allow it to subjugate us, we may be able to take our place among the confederations of the universe.

The global web of secret societies has multiplied, through bloodlines, into the highest level of the economic elite, which has manipulated populations through wars, plagues, economies, religions, politics and rumors (currently the media) for hundreds of years to further its ultimate goal: absolute power. War has been used in our time to develop technology and control economies.

✳   ✳   ✳

The esoteric knowledge from which secret powers were obtained was taught in the Egyptian and Babylonian mystery schools and the Hebrew Kabbalah. The teachings of the Knights Templar was taken up in Germany through the Thule Society, which was determined to unearth the power known and used in Atlantis. Many Germanic orders used Nazism to try to find Agartha (also called Shamballa), a paradise said to exist in the core of the planet. The German orders warred with the Brotherhoods of Zion, the modern capitalist Masons, the Freemasons and the Illuminati. World War II set the stage for the ancient orders to step up their pursuit of power and to discover Agartha/Shamballa.

Few people today know that a power grid surrounds Earth and extends through our universe. The Brotherhood orders have this secret knowledge, which was handed down through the ages. They have seized control of geomantic energy as one source of power. Their understanding of geomancy is shown in the placement of their structures and symbols. They have built the political centers of power in the past several hundred years. The geometries of the layout and the location of key government buildings in London, Paris and Washington, D.C., have harnessed Earth power; they are located on ley lines and nodes in Earth's energy grid and aligned with the cycles of Venus, the Sun, the Moon and other planets.

Using the male Sun cycles, these geometries and symbols capture the power of such sites to dominate the powers resident in the female polarity and female intelligence. Carefully placed phallic symbols dominate the female polarity, which is the womb of creation responsible for the evolution of humankind. The temples of the Brotherhood orders lay out symbols of the female organs— the womb, vagina and hymen—like wings of an angel, to be penetrated by the overpowering phallus, both symbolically and with literal geomantic energies.

The principle of the female was represented in ancient times by Venus, Isis, Ishtar, Noet, Sophia, Aphrodite, Kwan Yin, Sheba, White Buffalo Calf Woman, Spider Woman, Cihuacoatl and even the female Sphinx. The positive Moon

Goddess energy was actually advanced knowledge based on the feminine regenerative cycles of life.

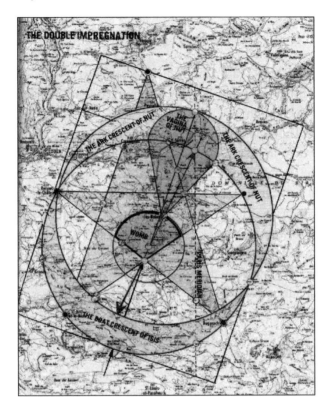

Fig. 36. The "Vagina of Nut".[4]

Our most ancient civilizations were matriarchal, and the most revered figure was a female oracle. Isis, Aphrodite and Athena were the keepers of mathematics, astronomy and medicine. Woman is the means for upgrading humankind, for it is she who, according to the Bible and ancient Vedic texts, copulated with the sky deities and produced modern man.

A war against Mother Earth is being waged by technology. We drill her, manipulate and dam her lakes and rivers so that her waters (her blood) cannot flow freely to heal her wounds, all for the Brotherhood orders' investment purposes. The blood sacrifice—the blood of woman, the blood of the flag, the blood ritual, the menstrual blood of the Virgin, the blood of Mother Earth— is in the wars the Brotherhood orders have been waging.

Women hold the key to life and regulate life through their blood. Mother Earth's waters are her blood, the life support system for all living creatures. A seed has no future unless the female cycle allows it. The Egyptian *thet* is the symbol of Isis and the instrument that elevates matter, energy, space and time into the theta universe, the eighth universe of pure thought. Isis thus holds the key of life and gives immortality to man.

When long ago men destroyed the power of the feminine, the feminine spirituality was lost to civilization, allowing the events that have come to pass. The violence done to Mother Earth and women throughout the world is a war being waged to destroy the feeling side of man so that he can be free to dismember the Earth and control the cosmos. The phallus of an unfeeling nuclear missile can destroy the cosmic womb.

Historically, women throughout the ages have had to separate from men to regain their power. This has happened in cycles on this planet; it is not a new war. But women do not go to war as men do. Women think with the right side of the brain, with love, birth and light—*Illuminari*. Men think with the left side of the brain, with logic, death and darkness—*Illuminati*. The sign of the beast, 666, is man himself, not the devil or Satan. Only through the unity of the masculine and feminine will balance and harmony be restored to life on this planet and throughout the omniverse. This cannot come about through the principles of a New World Order but through a spiritual transformation that begins from within.

In Egyptian mythology, depicted in ancient paintings, the boat of life carrying the Sun god Ra travels over the back of Nut as she bends over the Earth to shelter it. The key of life is the *crux ansata*, or ankh, the symbol for the rebirth of the ascending dimensions. This symbol is found on temples around the world, but particularly in Egypt. The secrets of matter, energy, time and space contain the order of the female mysteries. The female order is not only the source of life, but also the guardian of the knowledge that will transmute lower man into a being of higher intellect and even particlize matter into spirit.

Female intelligence is aligned with the Lords of Light and the Elder race, the Elohim, who are the true White Brotherhood from space. The Christ consciousness reveals itself through such avatars as Jesus Christ, Moses, Lord Krishna, Buddha, Saint Germain, Mohammed, Gandhi and Nelson Mandela, who teach compassion, unconditional love and forgiveness. The masters of space brought knowledge from an advanced civilization that has always assisted the evolution of humankind. The grand deception is to misinform humanity about this historical fact.

✳   ✳   ✳

© by Nancy Red Star.

Fig. 37. "The Wise Female Epoch" by Nancy Red Star.

Implanting higher knowledge came first through genetic breeding, which I believe the masters of space could have begun around 300,000 B.C. during a civilization on the earliest continent of Gondwanaland, which predates Lemuria, in what is called the "Wise Female" epoch.[5]

Gondwanaland was a continent on the southwestern coast of Africa where, some two or three hundred thousand years ago, a space-traveling Elder race from Sirius (the brightest star in the sky in the southern constellation Canis Major) began the biogenetic engineering of the Homo sapiens species to jump-start human evolution. (It is my understanding that these advanced civilizations had originally migrated from the central location of Lyra in the direction of the Pleiades.) The Sumerian reports explain that these races were created to mine gold.

Fig. 38. "Gondwanaland" by Christopher Schott.

This is not the area called E-din, for what we call Eden was located in southern Iraq, according to Sumerian records. Biologists have indeed traced humankind to a single woman in southern Africa somewhere between 170,000 to 250,000 years past. In his interpretations of the Sumerian records, Middle Eastern scholar Zecharia Sitchin questions the Nefilim as ancient heroes who, according to most interpreters, are the products of sexual union between heavenly beings and human women. In fact, according to Sitchin, the Nefilim and the Sumerian Anunnaki are one and the same. This is supported by the secret societies of Germany—the Thule Society and the Vril Society—who believed that there was a race who descended to Earth from Aldebaran and was called the Sumerians.[6]

According to literature in the Rosicrucian Library, the Hindu Indians are the purest blood of the Lemurians. In ancient Sanskrit (Vedic) texts, such as the *Ramayana* and the *Mahabharata*, we learn of space wars, flying machines and the Hanuman (a half monkey/half god interbreed), which could all be linked to the sky deities. Survivors of the sinking of Gondwanaland became what we know of as Lemuria, the second "Wise Female" epoch, which extended from today's Hawaiian Islands all the way to Easter Island in the Pacific. This migration was far-reaching during the last thousand years of Lemuria's existence; people migrated to North, Central and South America as well as to Africa, Egypt, India, Sumatra, Java, Borneo, New Guinea, Australia and New Zealand. This Lemurian culture was of the Illuminari order, which developed the qualities of the right-brained female intelligence. Its external and internal technology far exceeded that of today. The culture of Lemuria was perhaps the highest and most advanced civilization, as it was in harmony with the natural laws of light and matter, the harmonics of light.

Fig. 39. The god Hanuman.

Anthropological timelines show that the advanced culture of Lemuria was simultaneous with Stone Age man (the Neanderthals lived during the time of Atlantis). The Elder race again advanced evolution. The space beings used genetic engineering to mix Earth DNA with their own to create the Cro-Magnon and other species. This, I believe, began in Gondwanaland and continued through Lemuria to Atlantis. As it says in the Bible, "The sons of Gods saw the daughters of men that they were fair; and they took for them wives of all which they chose" (*Genesis 6:2*). This is the secret key to life here.

During the next great epoch, another culture arose on the continent of Atlantis. The main ceremonial center was located where the mid-Atlantic Ridge is today. The culture of Atlantis had advanced technological abilities, for they too had contact with the Lyran system, which had by this time migrated and built a substation on Mars.[7]

Fig. 40. Klamath Falls, California.[8]

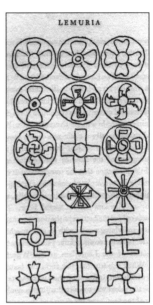

Fig. 41. Symbols of the Sacred Four.[9]

These early Earth cultures had begun many thousands of years before, with the strains of extraterrestrial ancestry held in female keeping. Not all humanoid extraterrestrial species were on the same level of advancement; some were the teachers of others, the keepers of knowledge through their advanced orders.

The continent of Atlantis survived for about thirty thousand years. Humankind once again transposed the extraterrestrial knowledge and science of life and matter through the harmonics of light—light technology. The subcultures of the Atlantean civilization that had been taught the secrets of science to assure the teachings' survival became vulnerable to ego demands for control. A conflict arose about the purpose and practical application of the science of light technology, and its eventual misuse came about through diabolical experiments.

In the latter days of Atlantis, the scientific and spiritual knowledge that had been collected from the ancient libraries of the Lemurian motherland through the mystery schools was hidden away for humankind's future evolution. These truths would be available when humans became spiritually awake.

❉　　　　　❉　　　　　❉

In contrast to the dark casts of the Brotherhood orders, we find in *Secret of the Andes,* by Brother Philip, that the true Great White Brotherhood is the original protector of the illumination of the seven rays.[10] The Brotherhood of Illumination, the Brotherhood of the Seven Rays, the Ancient Amethystine Order, the Order of the Red Hand and the Order of the Emerald Cross all work with the astral light of the seven rays vibration. This is the positive polarity of the Dark Brotherhood.

For thousands of years, the masters of other planets in space have been in communion with the master teachers on Earth. The original teachings of the mystery schools on Earth have been revealed through the Great White Brotherhood order, the protectors of the knowledge of the ancient truths. Central/South America is one location where the secrets have been protected. In the *Popol Vuh* it reads:

> We are going back to our own tribal place. Again it is the time of our Lord Deer, as is reflected in the sky. We have only to make our return. Our work has been done, our day has been completed. Since you know this, neither forget us nor put us aside. You have yet to see your own home and mountain, the place of your beginning.
>
> Let it be this way: you must go. Go see the place where we came from. . . . [11]

The Earth has entered into the vibration of the seventh great ray. The Brotherhood of Illumination, the Elder (El-der) race, or the "Els," are the Elohim of the violet frequency, where only truth shall survive. The Els are elevated to a dimension beyond time and space. The Brotherhood of the Seven Rays is the spiritual hierarchy of the true White Brotherhood from space—pure, harmonious and alive. The seven ray colors are red, light blue, green, yellow, indigo, rose and violet, and represent the natural laws of living—ceremony, devotion, arts, science, philosophy, education and leadership. These masters of space will assist us after the purification. They will not prevent this cleansing, but afterward they will land in great numbers. We must prepare for this—not with a missile defense shield, but with open hearts.

During the final Atlantean epoch, the mystery schools that originated in Lemuria migrated again to preserve their secret knowledge. At this time there

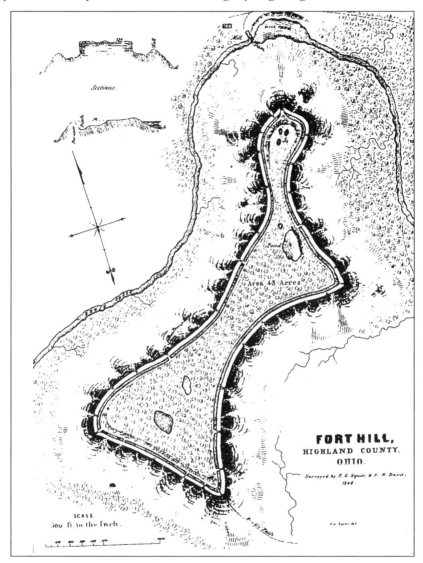

was a battle over the direction of the matriarchal female leadership. Some of the priestesses and priests carried the teachings by migrating to other continents.

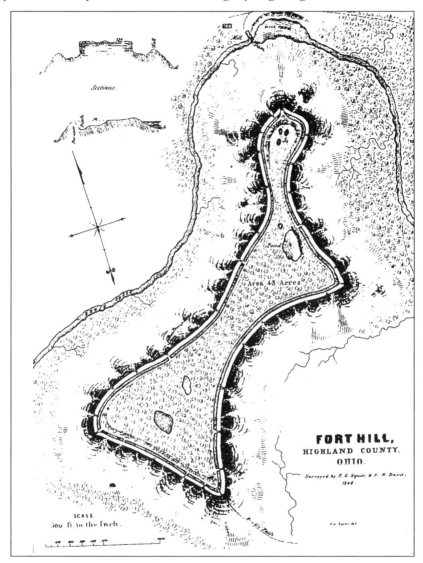

Fig. 42. The Serpent Mound—Adams County, Ohio.

This was the beginning of the Brotherhood of the Dragon. The symbol of the snake is derived from the regenerative power of the female, the "serpent wisdom," also seen in the yoga of the rising kundalini, in the Serpent Mound with its "egg" in Ohio, in the Aboriginal Rainbow Serpent and in the Feathered Serpent Quetzalcóatl, or Kukulcán.

According to the Maya, the original name for the Americas is Tamauanchan (Ta/Mauan/Chan), which means "land of the Eagle" (the male) and "land of the Serpent" (the female).[12] The restoration of unity to the polarities is symbolized by the caduceus, seen in both ancient and modern cultures.

The Brotherhood of the Dragon (snake or reptile) has always taken the secret knowledge from the ancient mystery schools and become the "black" force, the force of the Black Dragon, which still exists today. The battle is still waged between the male and female principles and among the secret societies themselves. The Middle East conflict has been instigated and expanded by the Illuminati (the New World Order's economic elite—international bankers, the war financiers), who orchestrate war for profit through oil and gold and drugs such as heroin and cocaine. But it also reflects the ancient struggle between the orders.[13]

The Brotherhood orders developed in Nazi Germany continued the battle, and the esoteric secrets that emerged from the Thule Society were simply rejuvenated ideas from the Crusades. At the close of World War II, the Black Sun's personnel were transferred into many scientific and intelligence agencies in

America. Some of the Brotherhood network and their secret orders were brought to the U.S. to jump-start the Star Wars project.

The manifesto of the Brotherhood orders is religious, political, economic and spiritual, controlling the banks, insurance companies, intelligence agencies, sciences and especially the media— anything that can keep the people under control. The "Sons of Darkness" are part of an order of the economic elite of any bloodline, be it Arab, Hebrew, Christian or Asian, because money, power and the belief in power will buy you entrance as an initiate to these orders.

Fig. 43. Good and evil battling for the universal egg.[14]

Take Hitler, for instance: When he came to power, his philosophy or goal was to bring the world into the Aquarian Age and the New World Order. Will we get a figurehead of compassion such as Jesus Christ to counteract Hitler? No, because someone like Jesus would never counteract someone like Hitler. We can see the works of the Brotherhood orders through the wars they create. Those who finance war back people like Hitler and Stalin simultaneously, and the worldwide web of the Brotherhood orders financed Hitler on one side and Stalin on the other. The international bankers knew that both men believed in dominating by eliminating their enemies. They were responsible for killing millions.

The shadow government financed Russia outwardly and Germany secretly so that it could maintain control. A problem is created so that someone is needed to solve it—Hitler and Stalin. This has always happened throughout the history of war. Abraham Lincoln believed in the Union and would go to war for that belief. John Brown rebelled and killed to free slaves. Both sides in the Civil War believed in war enough to kill their own brothers. Men have always been easily manipulated into waging war and still are today.

❋   ❋   ❋

My grandfather was a 33rd-degree Mason and my father was a Mason. I eventually recognized that the secret Brotherhood and the secret government were in partnership. How many of our leaders were part of this? George Washington, Thomas Jefferson and others who signed the Declaration of Independence to go to war with England were of the Brotherhood orders. We call those men who took the Constitution from the Iroquois Confederacy and called it their own idea our forefathers. If we look at the historical facts, we must admit that our history books are inaccurate at best, for the true forefathers of this continent are the American Indians. Where did they come from? Has that ever been accurately told? If you ask them, they will tell you they came from the stars; the Mesoamerican Indians, the Dogons, the Aboriginal people all claim descent from Sirius or the Pleiades. Their knowledge of star systems and cosmological symbols is represented in their structures, which are in astronomical alignment with the Sun and Moon. Furthermore, their ceremonies follow the movements of stars, and power was derived from this knowledge.

In modern times, as the American nation was being built, groups such as the Freemasons used powerful ancient symbols for the purpose of power and control. Their knowledge is reflected in their structures and in the sites' alignment with the energy grids, connecting them with the cosmos and the Sun and the Moon. Their fundamental symbol is the womb, upon which the Brotherhood orders have constructed their political temples. The womb might be considered a node in Mother Earth's power grid. The most powerful symbols are the egg (or dome), the phallus and the serpent, and through these the Brotherhood orders can manipulate humanity. When elongated the snake represents the phallus; when coiled it represents the egg and regeneration. Two snakes entwined around the winged staff, the caduceus, represent the knowledge of medicine, the union

of the female/male polarities and the generation of a third life. As H.P. Blavatsky, founder of the Theosophical Society, elaborates: "Before our globe had become egg-shaped or round, it was a long trail of cosmic dust or fire mist, moving and writhing like a serpent. This, say the explanations, was the Spirit of God moving on the chaos until its breath had incubated cosmic matter and made it assume the annular shape of a serpent with its tail in its mouth—emblem of eternity in its spiritual and our world in this physical sense."[15] But its basic meaning is the union of the space intelligences, the Lords of Light, with the female intelligence.

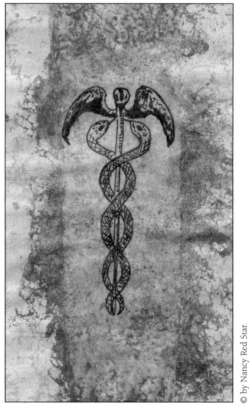

Fig. 44. "Caduceus" by Nancy Red Star.

The Pentagon is a huge five-sided building in Arlington, Virginia, head-quarters of the U.S. Department of Defense. It makes use of the power of the pentagon shape, a symbol from the Egyptian mystery schools. The pentagram employs the same energy of five, which symbolizes the female body and is embodied in the relation of Venus to the Sun. The six-pointed star represents the male. An inverted pentagram embodies the negative energy of the female, the center of which is the womb [see Fig. 46, the sigil of the beast]. Washington, D.C., the nation's political power center, was laid out in a reverse pentagram, which means that the congressional build-ing, the White House, the Washington Monument and so on represent and generate male dominion. These Masonic buildings are temples of the Brotherhood orders, whose symbols can be found throughout our planet. The intelligence agencies, the CIA, the National Reconnaissance Office (NRO), NATO, the fossil fuel industry and so on employ the energies of these esoteric symbols: the star, the cross, the circle and the all-seeing eye of the Great Pyramid.

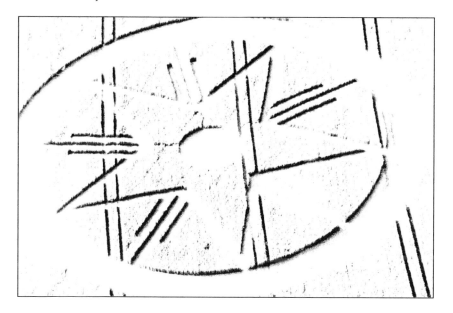

Fig. 45. A crop circle depicting the pentagram.

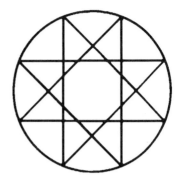

Fig. 46. The star of Isis and the sigil of the beast.[16]

In my study of history, I have come to the conclusion that women have always given life and men have taken it. Our current transition will return the female to a leadership role that will unify the polarities in a new coleadership. We are turning from the patriarchal toward the matriarchal for a restoration of balance. When cosmic consciousness fully arrives in the world, it will signal the successful union of the polarities. True healing will have taken place and peace will reign.

Today we see men struggling to integrate the feminine principle while women are coming forward to be wise leaders. In the teachings of the Lurianic Kabbalah, woman will always be a little higher than man because she is the crown above the head, nourished directly from overhead by the "Big Mother."[17]

Some would say that women cannot give life without men, but that is not true. We now know about the possibilities of genetic engineering, which need not be limited to the eggs and seeds of humans. It could include the seeds of an angel, a god or an extraterrestrial implanted in the dim past.

Every truly advanced civilization of the past literally disintegrated, moving from the fourth and fifth dimensions to the third. Sometimes they actually appeared or disappeared. They shifted like a figure eight from cycle to cycle, from beginning to end, like the symbol of a tetrahedron that merges two pyramids, one pointing up from the Earth and one pointing down from the heavens.

The extraterrestrials make themselves known at the end of one cycle and the beginning of another. An Elder race from space has always appeared during these epochal cycles. The goal is to continue evolving through the integration and healing symbolized by the serpent wisdom and the caduceus, the seven rays of astral light.

We should know this by now, but we have been asleep. Not only do we subconsciously know the meaning of these esoteric symbols, we have in our genetic memory the history of science. Electromagnetic energy, the technology of light, will bring us into the new age. We are being prepared for this now.

※　　　　　　　　※　　　　　　　　※

In New York City, Nikola Tesla demonstrated that generating free electricity was simple. Tesla's discovery of alternating current enabled the world's present electrical systems. Tesla claimed that during his experiments in the early 1900s in Colorado Springs, he'd made contact with advanced intelligence from off this planet. This also occurred when he created his transmitter on Long Island. Whatever help he got from extraterrestrials ultimately did us no good, because everyone who has made discoveries in the field of free energy has been bought out, intimidated, arrested or eliminated. Scientists have duplicated Tesla's experiments, but the economic elite and their partners, focused on profit and control, have so far successfully blocked them. That is how control is maintained.

The Brotherhood lodges are beginning to lose their power; that is the reason they are fearful. The governments are losing their power, too. Some in the Brotherhood understand why, because as the cycle progresses, people are getting smarter. We now know about the orders of the Brotherhood, the lodges, the NRO, MAJI, the Committee of Three Hundred, the International Council on Foreign Relations, the economic elite, the order of Skull and Bones, the Trilateral Commission, the Bilderbergs, the Brookings Institution and their history. We can research the history of their wars.

What will stop this struggle for control is the rediscovery of higher consciousness through the unification of polarized consciousness. I am hopeful that this will prevent World War III. We must experience a reawakening of consciousness. Thinking people know that we are not alone. The Elder race has crossed our path before; we both know that the other exists. These avatars are helping us to become aware, to remember the right and good and the truth, so we can enjoy peace for all ages, all sexes, all races. They have always come here to teach humanity.

There are unlimited omniverses and within each are thousands of universes. Because everything in those worlds consists of frequencies and wavelengths of energy, nuclear explosions can dissolve them. This will not be allowed, and much of the witness testimony of the Disclosure Project shows that in the past fifty years, ETVs have been seen over nuclear sites where we work on and store nuclear weapons.

The Brotherhood lodges are entering the time of purification through fire, and Hopi elder Thomas Banyaca says that we will see a time when the sky itself is on fire. The alchemist uses fire to extract pure gold. We can see this coming to pass today. When people are aware that the military intelligence agencies are at war with each other, then those agencies, under the Illuminati, will lose their power as they try to take over the oil and gold and drugs in Iraq and Afghanistan. We see this now. Only the truth can set us free. Will we choose the truth or the consequences?

Notes

1. David Wood, *Genisis: The First Book of Revelations* (Kent, England: Baton Press, 1985), 32.
2. Ibid., 78.
3. For more information, see Joscelyn Godwin, trans., *The Chemical Wedding of Christian Rosenkreutz*, (Kimball, Mich.: Phanes Press, 1991).
4. Wood, *Genisis*, 27.
5. Valdamar Valerian, *Matrix IV: The Equivideum, Paradigms & Dimensions of Human Evolution and Consciousness* (Yelm, Wash.: Leading Edge, 1994), 57.
6. Zecharia Sitchin, *The 12th Planet* (Rochester, Vt.: Bear & Company, 1977).
7. Using NASA photos, Richard Hoagland has overlaid the Egyptian Sphinx and Giza pyramids upon the area on Mars named Cydonia, showing that this site contains exactly the same geometries, as well as that of megalithic sites in England and South America. This was the same advanced Elder race that continued to genetically engineer strains of Earth inhabitants.
8. Wishar S. Cervé, *Lemuria: The Lost Continent of the Pacific*, vol.xii (San Jose: Rosicrucian Press, 1931), 242.
9. Ibid., 174.
10. Brother Philip [George Hunt Williamson], *Secret of the Andes* (Bolinas,Calif.: Leaves of Grass Press, 1976).

11. Dennis Tedlock, trans., *Popol Vuh: The Definitive Edition of the Mayan Book of the Dawn of Life and the Glories of Gods and Kings* (New York: Simon and Schuster, 1958), 197–198.

12. Nancy Red Star, *Star Ancestors: Indian Wisdomkeepers Share the Teachings of the Extraterrestrials* (Rochester, Vt.: Destiny Books, 2000), 92.

13. For more information, see the following books by David Icke: *Alice in Wonderland and the World Trade Center Disaster: Why the Official Story of 9/11 Is a Monumental Lie* (Ryde, Isle of Wight: Bridge of Love Publications, 2002); *The Biggest Secret: The Book That Will Change the World,* second edition (Ryde, Isle of Wight: Bridge of Love Publications, 1999);
Children of the Matrix: How an Interdimensional Race Has Controlled the World for Thousands of Years—And Still Does (Ryde, Isle of Wight: Bridge of Love Publications, 2001); and . . . *And the Truth Shall Set You Free: The Most Explosive Book of the 20th Century* (Ryde, Isle of Wight: Bridge of Love Publications, 1998).

14. Manly P. Hall, *The Secret Teachings of All Ages: An Encyclopedic Outline of Masonic, Hermetic, Qabbalistic & Rosicrucian Symbolical Philosophy* (Los Angeles: Philosophical Research Society, 1928), ixxxviii.

15. Helena Petrovna Blavatsky, *Isis Unveiled* (Pasadena, Calif.: Theosophical University Press, 1999).

16. David Wood, *Genisis,* 134–135, 228.

17. Nancy Red Star, *Legends of the Star Ancestors: Stories of Extraterrestrial Contact from Wisdomkeepers around the World* (Rochester, Vt.: Destiny Books, 2002), Chapter 2.

CHAPTER EIGHT

STAR WARS

The first sighting I and my crew had was of three extraterrestrial craft on top of the radar tower at Warner Robbins Air Force Base in Georgia. Seeing the zero acknowledgment and blackout of the report, I then suspected that the Air Force and CIA were covering up more incidents. That is when I began my own search and was convinced that other people were also having encounters. One of my areas of research became the industrial-military complex. The innards of the beast and the complex that feeds it became my main interest thereafter.

Star Wars, which is popularly thought of as a missile defense system, is known within the military as the Space Defense Initiative (SDI). The prime directive from the Extraterrestrial Network given to governments throughout the world states: "There will be no interference with an emerging extraterrestrial population or race of people." What the Network's directive means is that without being asked, no nation, military complex or government will interfere with the development or evolutionary progress of a race from another planet or solar system. For instance, if the U.S. found a planet and wanted to develop life there, if nobody else lived there, then that planet would have no laws and we could establish our own. But if another extraterrestrial race inhabited that planet, the U.S. could not interfere.

Space laws were drafted in 1947 by the U.S. at the highest levels, proposing our views. These views were initially developed in a letter entitled "Relationships with Inhabitants of Celestrial Bodies" [sic], which was sent in June 1947 from Dr. J. Robert Oppenheimer, Director of Advanced Studies at Princeton, to Professor Albert Einstein, also at Princeton.[1]

✳   ✳   ✳

> **IUP SECRET**   JUN 47
>
> ────────────────────────────
>
> DRAFT   June 1947
>
> **Relationships with Inhabitants
> of Celestrial Bodies**
>
> Relationships with extraterrestrial men presents no bascially new problem from the standpoint of international law; but the possibility of confronting intelligent beings that do not belong to the human race would bring up problems whose solution it is difficult to conceive.
>
> In principle, there is no difficulty in accepting the possibility of coming to an understanding with them, and of establishing all kinds of relationships. The difficulty lies in trying to establish the principles on which these relationships should be based.
>
> In the first place, it would be necessary to establish communication with them through some language or other, and afterwards, as a first condition for all intelligence, that they should have a psychology similar to that of men.
>
> At any rate, international law should make place for a new law on a different basis, and it might be called "Law Among Planetary Peoples," following the guidelines found in the Pentateuch. Obviously, the idea of revolutionizing international law to the point where it would be capable of coping with new situations would compel us to make a change in its structure, a change so basic that it would no longer be international law, that is to say, as it is conceived today, but something altogether different, so that it could no longer bear the same name.
>
> If these intelligent beings were in possession of a more or less culture, and a more or less perfect political organization, they would have an absolute right to be recognized as independent and soverign peoples, we would have to come to an agreement with them to establish the legal regulations upon which future relationships should be based, and it would be necessary to accept many of their principles.
>
> Finally, if they should reject all peaceful cooperation and become an imminent threat to the earth, we would have the right to legitimate defense, but only insofar as would be necessary to annul this danger.
>
> ✦✦✦✦✦
>
> Another possibility may exist, that a species of homo sapiens might have established themselves as an independent nation on another celestrial body in our solar system and
>
> -1-

Fig. 47. Letter from Dr. J. Robert Oppenheimer to Albert Einstein—Part 1.

evolved culturely indenpendently from ours. Obviously, this
possibility depends on many circumstances, whose conditions
cannot yet be foreseen. However, we can make a study of the
basis on which such a thing might have occurred.

In the first place, living conditions on these bodies
lets say the moon, or the planet Mars, would have to be such
as to permit a stable, and to a certain extent, independent
life, from an economic standpoint. Much has been speculated
about the possibilities for life existing outside of our
atmosphere and beyond, always hypothetically, and there are
those who go so far as to give formulas for the creation of
an artificial atmosphere on the moon, which undoubtedly have
a certain scientific foundation, and which may one day come
to light. Lets assume that magnesium silicates on the moon
may exist and contain up to 13 per cent water. Using energy
and machines brought to the moon, perhaps from a space station,
the rocks could be broken up, pulverized, and then backed to
drive off the water of crystallization. This could be collected
and then decomposed into hydrogen and oxygen, using an electric
current or the short wave radiation of the sun. The oxygen
could be used for breathing purposes; the hydrogen might be
used as a fuel.

In any case, if no existence is possible on celestrial
bodies except for enterprises for the exploration of their
natural riches, with a continuous interchange of the men who
work on them, unable to establish themselves there indefinitely
and be able to live isolated life, independence will never
take place.

*****

Now we come to the problem of determining what to
do if the inhabitants of clestrial bodies, or extraterrestrial
biological entities (EBE) desire to settle here.

1. If they are politically organized and possess a
certain culture similar to our own, they may be recognized as
a independent people. They could consider what degree of
development would be required on earth for colonizing.

2. If they consider our culture to devoid of political
unity, they would have the right to colonize. Of course, this
colonization cannot be conducted on classic lines.

A superior form of colonizing will have to be conceived,
that could be a kind of tutelage, possibly through the tacit
approval of the United Nations. But would the United Nations
legally have the right of allowing such tutelage over us in such
a fashion?

-2-

Fig. 47. Part 2.

TOP SECRET

(a) Although the United Nations is an
international organization, there is no doubt that it would
have no right of tutelage, since its domain does not extend
beyond relationships between its members. It would have the
right to intervene only if the relationships of a member
nation with a celestrial body affected another member nation
with an extraterrestrial people is beyond the domain of the
United Nations. But if these relationships entailed a
conflict with another member nation, the United Nations would
have the right to intervene.

(b) If the United Nations were a supra-national
organization, it would have competency to deal with all
problems related to extraterrestrial peoples. Of course,
even though it is merely an international organization, it
could have this competence if its member states would be
willing to recognize it.

*****

It is difficult to predict what the attitude of
international law will be with regard to the occupation by
celestrial peoples of certain locations on our planet, but
the only thing that can be foreseen is that there will be
a profound change in traditional concepts.

We cannot exclude the possibility that a race of
extraterrestrial people more advanced technologically and
economically may take upon itself the right to occupy
another celestrial body. How, then, would this occupation
come about?

1. The idea of exploitation by one celestrial
state would be rejected, they may think it would be advisable
to grant it to all others capable of reaching another
celestrial body. But this would be to maintain a situation
of privilege for these states.

2. The division of a celestrail body into zones
and the distribution of them among other celestrial states.
This would present the problem of distribution. Moreover,
other celestrial states would be deprived of the possibility
of owning an area, or if they were granted one it would
involve complicated operations.

3. Indivisible co-sovereignty, giving each celestrial
state the right to make whatever use is most convenient to
its interests, independently of the others. This would
create a situation of anarchy, as the strongest one would
win out in the end.

4. A moral entity? The most feasible solution it

-3-

Fig. 47. Part 3.

TOP SECRET

704

seem would be this one, submitt an agreement providing for the peaceful absorbtion of a celestrial race(s) in such a manner that our culture would remain intact with guarantees that their presence not be revealed.

Actually, we do not believe it necessary to go that far. It would merely be a matter of internationalizing celestrial peoples, and creating an international treaty intsrument preventing exploitation of all nations belonging to the United Nations.

*****

Occupation by states here on earth, which has lost all interest for international law, since there were no more **res** _nullius_ territories, is beginning to regain all its importance in cosmic international law.

Occupation consists in the appropriation by a state of **res** _nullius_.

Until the last century, occupation was the normal means of acquiring sovereignty over territories, when explorations made possible the discovery of new regions, either unihabited or in an elementary state of civilization.

The imperialist expansion of the states came to an end with the end of regions capable of being occupied, which have now been drained from the earth and exist only in interplanetary space, where the celestrial states present new problems.

*****

Res _nullius_ is something that belongs to nobody such as the moon. In international law a celestrial body is not subject to the sovereignty of any state is considered **res** _nullius_. If it could be established that a celestrial body within our solar system such as our moon was, or is occupied by another celestrial race, there could be no claim of **res** _nullius_ by any state on earth (if that state should decide in the future to send explorers to lay claim to it). It would exist as **res** _communis_, that is that all celestrial states have the same rights over it.

*****

And now to the final question of whether the presence of celestrial astroplanes in our atmosphere is a direct result of our testing atomic weapons?

The presence of unidentified space craft flying in our atmosphere (and possibly maintaining orbits about our planet) is now, however, accepted ░░ by our military.

-4-   *usdefacto*

Fig. 47. Part 4.

TOP SECRET

On every question of whether the United States will continue testing of fission bombs and develop fusion devices (hydrogen bombs), or reach an agreement to disarm and the exclusion of weapons that are too destructive, with the exception of chemical warfare, on which, by some miracle we cannot explain, an ▄▄ agreement has been reached, the lamentations of philosophers, the efforts of politicians, and the conferences of diplomats have been doomed to failure and have accomplished nothing.

The use of the atomic bomb combined with space vehicles poses a threat on a scale which makes it absolutely necessary to come to an agreement in this area. With the appearance of unidentified space vehicles (opinions are sharply divided as to their origin) over the skies of Europe and the United States has sustained an ineradical fear, an anxiety about security, that is driving the great powers to make an effort to find a solution to the threat.

Military strategists foresee the use of space craft with nuclear warheads as the ultimate weapon of war. Even the deployment of artificial satellites for intelligence gathering and target selection is not far off. The military importance of space vehicles, satellites as well as rockets is indisputable, since they project war from the horizontal plane to the vertical plane in its fullest sense. Attack no longer comes from an exclusive direction, nor from a determined country, but from the sky, with the practical impossibility of determining who the aggressor is, how to intercept the attack, or how to effect immediate reprisals. These problems are compounded further by identification. How does the air defense radar operator identify , or more precisely, classify his target?

At present, we can breath a little easier knowing that slow moving bombers are the mode of delivery of atomic bombs that can be detected by long-range early warning radar. But what do we do in lets say ten years from now? When artificial satellites and missiles find their place in space, we must consider the potential threat that unidentified space craft pose. One must consider the fact that mis-identification of these space craft for a intercontenental missile in a re-entry phase of flight could lead to accidental nuclear war with horrible consequences.

Lastly, we should consider the possibility that our atmospheric tests of late could have influenced the arrival of celestrial scrutiny. They could have been curious or even alarmed by such activity (and rightly so, for the Russians would make every effort to observe and record such tests).

In conclusion, it is our professional opinion based on submitted data that this situation is extremely perilous, and

-5-

Fig. 47. Part 5.

TOP SECRET

measures must be taken to rectify a very serious problem are
very apparent.

Respectfully,

/s/

Dr. J. Robert Oppenheimer

Director of Advanced Studies
Princeton, New Jersey

/s/

Professor Albert Einstein

Princeton, New Jersey

Myself and Marshall have read this and I must admit there
is some logic. But I hardly think the President will consider
it for the obvious reasons. I understand Oppenheimer
approached Marshall while they attended ceremony at
        As I understand it Marshall rebuffed the idea
of Oppenheimer discussing this with the President. I talked
to Gordon, and he agreed.

-6-

Fig. 47. Part 6.

As we now know, after Roswell and after MAJI, Majestic 12 was formally established by a presidential classified order in September 1947. This group and its operations were classified as Top Secret and reported only to President Truman. Later, members of this group came to be called the Wise Elders.

In December 1947, Truman approved Project NSC-4, the Coordination of Foreign Intelligence Information Measures, at the urging of Secretaries George C. Marshall, Robert P. Patterson and George F. Kennan from the State Department's Policy Group and Secretary of Defense James Forrestal, who had actually seen the extraterrestrials and was against the measures being taken to cover up the secret of their presence.

Forrestal was a good man who wanted to expose the truth. He was asked to resign by Truman and was subsequently imprisoned in a military hospital. The world was told that he'd had a nervous breakdown, but his two brothers retained lawyers who demanded his release. The lawyers were successful, and the paperwork was approved. But the night before his release, agents broke into his room, took a sheet and a rope, tied it around his neck and threw him out the window. The rope broke. The fall did not kill him, but he was assassinated immediately, right there on the ground, and his death was declared a suicide. Forrestal was the first person executed to keep UFO information secret, even though he was one of the original members of the Majestic 12 group. As the Majestic 12 group's Special Operations Manual [see Fig. 52, Part 2] states: "MJ-12 takes the subject of UFOBs, Extraterrestrial Technology, and Extraterrestrial Biological Entities very seriously and considers the entire subject to be a matter of the very highest national security."

Certain rules that every species is supposed to abide by already exist. If a nation interferes with another planet's domain, it will come upon these laws. The prime directive was given to us by the Extraterrestrial Network, and Eisenhower signed a treaty to this effect. All the extraterrestrial races we have had physical contact with warned us not to use nuclear weapons, especially not in space, because they interfere with other worlds we are not even aware of.

TOP SECRET
EYES ONLY
THE WHITE HOUSE
WASHINGTON

September 24, 1947.

MEMORANDUM FOR THE SECRETARY OF DEFENSE

Dear Secretary Forrestal:

As per our recent conversation on this matter, you are hereby authorized to proceed with all due speed and caution upon your undertaking. Hereafter this matter shall be referred to only as Operation Majestic Twelve.

It continues to be my feeling that any future considerations relative to the ultimate disposition of this matter should rest solely with the Office of the President following appropriate discussions with yourself, Dr. Bush and the Director of Central Intelligence.

Harry Truman

HQ Interplanetary Phenomenon
Scientific and Technical
C.... Intelligence Unit
.... D.C.

Fig. 48. Truman memo.

I have never seen this document, which I believe was officially consummated, but in the Disclosure Project I heard the testimony of Don Phillips, who, again, was a CIA contractor for the Lockheed Skunkworks. He has actually seen the film of the meeting between the extraterrestrials and high-ranking U.S. officials at a site in California. Where and how he got to see this film Don was unable to disclose.

I consider Don Phillips to be a brilliant man, on the level of Nikola Tesla. He has proven this with the technologies developed by his corporation, Light City Technology. These technologies can eliminate environmental pollutants and our need for fossil fuels. He also developed a prototype of an advanced energy system using electromagnetic energy that can run an entire city. In fact, he has developed numerous patented technologies to move us into the new world. This is what we need to be doing now. If we are not part of the solution, we become part of the problem.

The treaty with the ETs grew out of what happened at Roswell, New Mexico. I heard testimonies at the Disclosure Project from officials who were present at Roswell and consequently knew of this agreement and how it came about. Philip Corso Jr. testified that his father, Col. Philip Corso Sr., who served in Army Intelligence on Eisenhower's National Security Council, personally saw the extraterrestrials from the Roswell crash and their vehicles. Corso Jr. stated further that his father had been involved in high-level meetings and discussions surrounding the extraterrestrial subject with such people as FBI director J. Edgar Hoover, President Eisenhower and Wernher von Braun. When Corso Sr. was working at the White House, he was part of a new research and development project. Out of this group came the Foreign Technology Division, through which he began receiving autopsy reports from Walter Reed Hospital as well as recovered artifacts.

Corso Jr. testified that the SDI is really a planetary defense system set up to protect the planet from extraterrestrial races. Those in the military knew this, but in the testimonies of the government personnel at the Disclosure Project we learned that the extraterrestrials can and do shut down our nuclear missiles and warheads both in airspace and where they are stored and manufactured. As discussed earlier, this means that we will be prevented from successfully weaponizing space, even if we try.

During the Cold War, some nations questioned the right of the United Nations to have authority over the space laws. But some organization, like the United Nations, for example, may have to draw up an agreement for the extraterrestrials when they arrive. In 1947, after the Roswell incident, Majestic 12 began to draw up laws for outer-space discoveries and possible occupation by extraterrestrial beings, who had contacted numerous governments around the world. This means that in 1947, we in the scientific and technical units of interplanetary phenomena were trying to find ways to deal with and administer the laws governing extraterrestrial races who might want to be on this planet. We wanted to establish laws to govern this planet, for our nation as well as for any other nation that might have such contact. This draft not only tells what the laws might be, it also questions what would happen if extraterrestrials would not abide by these laws.

After 1947, Majestic 12 became the UFO policy group, whose function was to investigate and to administer these laws if an extraterrestrial race decided to reside here. Dr. Oppenheimer and Professor Einstein were consultants of MJ-12. Against the recommendation of the Extraterrestrial Network and the Greada Treaty we signed, the U.S. continued to develop nuclear weapons because MJ-12 feared that we would need them in outer space.

In the analysis of Sky Watch, the Star Wars intelligence organization, the 1010 Special Security Squadron reported to the National Reconnaissance Office (NRO) and to MAJI. It bypassed the Air Force, the Army, the Navy and the Defense Department.[2] Projects Blue Book, Grudge, Snowbird and all UFO and space intelligence agencies were spied on by the NRO. That is how Eisenhower developed policy through MJ-12.

Eisenhower was the Supreme Commander of the Allied Forces during WWII and knew the importance and power of intelligence. But he left office with a warning to the people; he knew the elected government had lost control of the military-industrial complex, because the secret government put in place during his administration secured that control for their own goals. "Top Secret Eyes Only" was for those in the secret government who designed the policies we now live under.

TOP SECRET

ULTRA

INTERPLANETARY PHENOMENON UNIT SUMMARY

INTELLIGENCE ASSESSMENT File ref. 001947122-A.1206

1. The extraordinary recovery of fallen airborne objects in the state of New Mexico, between 4 July - 6 July 1947. This Summary was prepared by Headquarters Interplanetary Phenomenon Unit, Scientific and Technical Branch, Counterintelligence Directorate, as requested by A.C. of S., G-2, at the expressed order of Chief of Staff.

2. At 2312 MSI, 3 July 47, radar stations in east Texas and White Sands Proving Ground, N.M., tracked two unidentified aircraft until both dropped off radar. Two crash sites have been located close to the WSPG. Site LZ-1 was located at a ranch near Corona, approx. 75 miles northwest of the town of Roswell. Site LZ-2 was located approx. 20 miles southeast of the town of Socorro, at Lat. 33-40-31, Long. 106-28-29, with Oscura Peak being the geographic reference point.

3. The AST personnel were mainly interested in LZ-2 as this site contained the majority of structural detail of the craft's airframe, propulsion and navigation technology. The recovery of five bodies in a damaged escape cylinder, precluded an investigation at LZ-1.

4. On arrival at LZ-2, personnel assessed the finds as not belonging to any aircraft, rocket, weapons, or balloon test that are normally conducted from surrounding bases. First reports indicated that the first crash investigators from Roswell AAF that LZ-1 was the remains of a AAF top secret MOGUL balloon project. When scientists

-2-

TOP SECRET

Fig. 49. Interplanetary Phenomenon Unit Summary—Part 1.

ULTRA

from the Los Alamos Scientific Laboratory arrived to inspect IZ-2, it became apparent to all concerned that what had crashed in the desert was something out of this world.

5. Interviews with radar operators and officers from the Signal Corps Engineering Laboratories, Fort Monmouth, N.J., who were tracking these objects on-and-off since June 29 from Station "A", all indicated that these targets had periodically remained stationary for minutes at a time, then would resume thier original course, flying from the southeast to northwest. SCEL antennas had locked onto a flight of three objects on 3 July and lost them around 2330 MST on 4 July (a V-2 was scheduled for launch which is why SCEL Station "A" was able to do a track). It has been learned that at least six radar stations in east Texas (see detailed report in attchment A), and radar stations at Alamogordo AAF and Kirtland AAF, had also picked up these objects on the 4th as well. Using topographical maps and triangularization, a last known position and bearing was calculated which helped search parties to locate the general area. Detachment 3 of the 9393rd Technical Services Unit, assigned to Alamogordo AAF, was responsible for the locating and transportation of the larger sections of the craft.

6. A special radiobiological team accompanied by a SED and security detail from Sandia Base under orders from Colonel S. V. /HASBROUCK/ USA, Armed Forces Special Weapons Project, secured the immediate area surrounding the crash site. Select scientists from

-3-

TOP SECRET

ULTRA

ULTRA

the General Advisory Committee of the Atomic Energy Commission, most notably DR. J. ROBERT OPPENHEIMER, was identified at LZ-2 as well as other members. Among PAPERCLIP specialist identified at LZ-2 were DR. WERNHER VON BRAUN (Fort Bliss); DR. ERNST STEINHOFF (AMC); and DR. HUBERTUS STRUGHOLD (AEROMEDICAL LAB, RANDOLPH FIELD).

7. Because of the stringent security measures that were in place at both crash sites, the team was not able to gain access to the several locations were wreckage and bodies are being held. CIC member of the team was able to learn that several bodies were taken to the hospital at Roswell AAF and others to either Los Alamos, Wright Field, Patterson AAF, and Randolph Field for security reasons. It is believed that this dispersion was on the orders of General Thomas Handy, Fourth Army Hdqrs. Remains of the powerplant were taken to Alamogordo AAF and Kirtland AAF. Structural debris and assorted parts were taken to AMC, Wright Field. Other remains were transported across the WSPG to the storage facilities of the NRL. All this was accomplished by 1730 MST 7 July.

8. On 7 July, Lt. General Nathan Twining arrived at Alamogordo AAF for a secret meeting with AAF Chief of Staff Spaatz and to view recovered remains of craft from LZ-2. On 8 July, Twining visited Kirtland AAF to inspect parts recovered from powerplant. On 9 July, Twining and staff flew to WSPG to inspect pieces of craft being stored there and on 10 July, made inspection of R&D facilities at Alamogordo and then returned to Wright Field. It is believed that Twining and staff is preparing a detailed report of both incidents and briefings later to follow. It is also the belief of CIC that General Eisenhower will see a showing of recoveries sometime in late August this year. The President was given a limited briefing

—4—

Fig. 49. Part 3.

ULTRA

at the Pentagon by AC/S AAF General Hoyt Vandenberg on 15

interest was curtailed and access to stored craft at Los Alamos was
denied upon request of Deputy COS Lt. General Collins. Inquiries to
bases involved was restricted by General Vandenberg during the duration
of recovery efforts. All teletype, telephone and radio transmissions
were monitored for any disclosures of the finds. To maintain secrecy
of site LZ-2, the CO of Roswell AAF was authorized to give a brief
press release to local paper in which 8th AF Hdqrs. promptly denied
rumors that the Army had flying saucers in their possession which
effectively killed press interest. Civilians who might have seen or
handled some of the wreckage, or viewed bodies were detained under the
McNab law until all remaing evidence was secured in restricted bases.
Witnesses were debriefed by CIC and warned of the consequences of
talking to the press. So far, secrecy seems to be working.

9.   All civilian and military personnel involved with the
recovery operations had "need to know" access with proper security
clearances. Though several MPs suffered nervous breakdowns resulting in
one committing suicide, MP details from Alamogordo and Kirtland performed
security functions very well. Ground personnel from Sandia experienced
some form of contamination resulting in the deaths of 3 technicians.
The status of the fourth technician is unknown. Autopsies are scheduled
to determine cause of death. CIC has made appropriate security file
entries into dossiers with cross references for future reviews.

10.   With the pending approval of JAMES FORRESTAL as new
Secretary of Defense, it is certain that he will be briefed on certain
aspects of the discoveries. The only Cabinet member to date that may
know of the details is Secretary of State Marshall. It has become known
to CIC that some of the recovery operation was shared with Representative

-5-

Fig. 49. Part 4.

ULTRA

/JOHN F. KENNEDI,/Massachusetts Democrat elected to Congress in 46. Son of JOSEPH P. KENNEDI, Commission on Organization of the Executive Branch of the Government. KENNEDI had limited duty as naval officer assigned to Naval Intelligence during war. It is believed that information was obtained from source in Congress who is close to Secretary for Air Force.

11. As to the bodies recovered at LZ-2, it appeared that none of the five crew members survived entry into our atmosphere due to unknown causes. /DR. DETLEV BRONK/ has been asked to assist in the autopsy of one well preserved cadaver to be done by MAJOR CHARLES E. REA. From what descriptions the team was able to learn and from photographs taken by intelligence photographers', the occupants appear in most respects human with /some anatomical differences/ in the head, eyes, hands and feet. They have a slight build about five feet tall, with grayish-pink skin color. They have no hair on their bodies and clothed with a tight fitting flight suit that appears to be fire proof (some of the bodies looked as if they had been burned on head and and hands). Their overall stature reminds one of /young children./ It is believed that there were male and female genders present, but was hard to distinguish.

12. The most disturbing aspect of this investigation was— there were other bodies found not far from LZ-1 that looked as if they had been disected as you would a frog. It is not known if army field surgens had performed exploratory surgery on these bodies. Animal parts were reportedly discovered inside the craft at LZ-2 but this cannot be confirmed. The team has reserved judgement on this issue.

13. Our assessment of this investigation rests on two assumptions: 1) Either this discovery was an elaborate and well orchestrated hoax (maybe by the Russians), or; 2) Our country has played host to

-6-

Fig. 49. Part 5

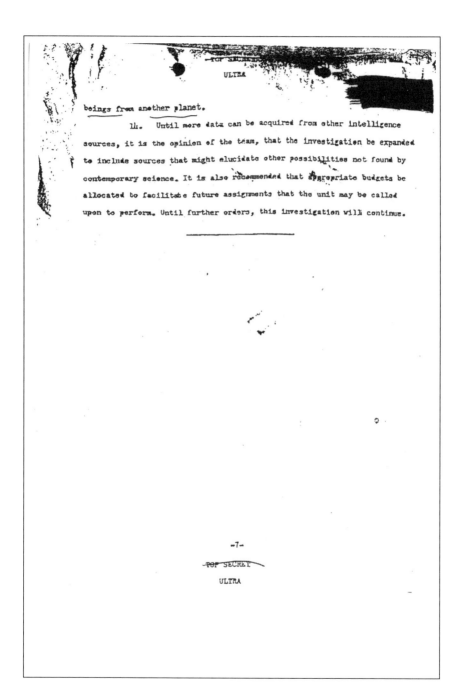

beings from another planet.

14. Until more data can be acquired from other intelligence sources, it is the opinion of the team, that the investigation be expanded to include sources that might elucidate other possibilities not found by contemporary science. It is also recommended that appropriate budgets be allocated to facilitate future assignments that the unit may be called upon to perform. Until further orders, this investigation will continue.

-7-

TOP SECRET

ULTRA

Fig. 49. Part 6

Our government has been continually warned by the ET Network not to use plutonium in our missiles, and whenever we did this, they neutralized them or blew them up. Building nuclear weapons keeps people occupied and builds a defense system—but against whom? Against the Extraterrestrial Network? That cannot work. What is the resistance to accepting that the ETs' capability by far exceeds that of our military? The military-industrial complex does not want anybody to have power over it. It has nothing to do with our human evolution, only with power and money—with control. The Extraterrestrial Network has never quarantined us, never told us not to travel in space; the ETs have only told us not to use nuclear weapons in space. But we haven't listened.[3]

Having been in the federal service for more than forty years, I am familiar with how the military thinks and operates. When in service, one learns not to interfere. If you do, you pay—one way or another. This is not to say that all military people or even all nations agree with our weaponized space program, which is fundamentally built from the Star Wars program.

✳   ✳   ✳

The "coldest warriors" were members of the NRO; they are buried deeply in secrecy and answer to no one. I don't agree with this, especially when the information bypasses the president and Congress. Eisenhower was the closest to the intelligence operations of the NRO; he had insisted upon its conception that it be independent and civilian. The NRO became fully independent around 1960 or 1961. Until that time, it was under the CIA and Naval, Air Force and Army Intelligence. They had all worked together at Langley Field in Virginia.

One of the purposes of the NRO was to manage the spy planes and satellites under a National Reconnaissance Program. The U-2, the Blackbird and other secret airplanes reported to the NRO. A month after Russia shot down Gary Powers in our U-2 spy plane near Svedlovsk in the Soviet Union, the U.S. launched its first spy satellite. Corona was the code name it was given. The U-2 was a supersonic plane built the same year as the Oxcart A-12 spy plane. We now have the Predator, an unmanned aerial vehicle (UAV) with cameras on board, which goes higher and faster.[4] We are also developing a microflyer used for spying called the Robofly, a UAV the size of a fly with a camera on board. Now where do you think we got this technology from?

All the technologies that have been developed have pockets that are very deep, very black and void of any red tape or congressional oversight. President Eisenhower ordered the creation of the NRO after the first Corona mission because he was aware of the interservice conflicts that had helped defeat Germany when each service competed for military contracts. He wanted the Office of Strategic Services (OSS) to ensure that the programs served the nation rather than only the military. He knew that the development of programs like the Corona had become veiled because advanced extraterrestrial technologies were secretly being used. On the outside, the NRO was created with three separate divisions, developing satellites (1) for the CIA, managing the Agency's air operations; (2) for the Navy and its ocean reconnaissance; and (3) for all military aircraft.

But the "black" part inside the NRO controlled and collected information via world spy satellites on all UFO activity entering or leaving the Earth's atmosphere. It instructed the military on the use of all beam weaponry from the Star Wars program to effectively disrupt or dismantle any and all extraterrestrial vehicles. The NRO and its military intelligence programs were formed to retrieve, capture and interrogate extraterrestrial biological entities and extraterrestrial vehicles in the name of national security. Part of the strategy was to mock human abductions utilizing mind control or National Security Agency (NSA) hypnotic scripting for the purpose of a public disinformation campaign to create fear regarding extraterrestrial encounters. The CIA works with the NSA and the NRO on these Black Projects, to be in control of exactly what information is going out into the public arena via the strong arm of the accomplice media.

The Corona project was the first time the U.S. put cameras in space; we shot monkeys into space as a disguise. When the project went through, nobody guessed there had been a camera on board. But when President Eisenhower showed President Khrushchev the high-altitude photos of his country, soon thereafter Russia also had cameras in space. President Khrushchev is the one who later exposed the secret of Area 51 to Dan Rather.

Eisenhower never wanted the military and industrial powers to collude; he knew that would violate our Constitution. (When I say "military and industrial powers," what I'm talking about is the Illuminati.) We now have a form of government that does exactly that, even though it is supposed to be run by civilians. The NRO was supposed to be run by civilians, but the two people who directed the NRO in 1961 were Richard Bissell, the CIA's deputy director, and the Undersecretary of the Air Force, Joseph V. Charyk. This did not work, so the incoming Kennedy administration made Charyk the sole director, eliminating the CIA faction. In 1962, the NRO was in conflict with the Department of Defense, the CIA and the Air Force. From then on, everything the NRO did was veiled in secrecy; nothing was shared. Nobody even knew it existed; officially it did not exist until 1997. The coverup came out of the Pentagon, from what was called the Office of Space Systems.

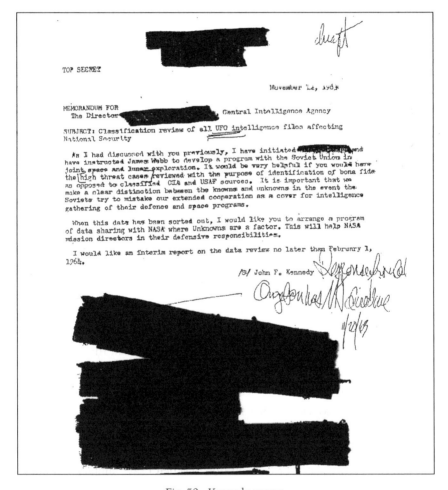

Fig. 50. Kennedy memo.

The Star Wars City chart [see Fig. 51] shows how the U.S. Space Counterintelligence Headquarters works. The NRO reports directly to the president concerning certain subjects only. It also reports to MAJI. MAJI will brief the president only on some matters. Note that the NRO receives most of its reports from the 1010 Special Security Squadron.

The next level is the National Security Council (NSC), which is made up of representatives from all the security agencies. With the advice of the NRO, the NSA is supposed to make and enforce policy. Then we have the Director of Central Intelligence (DCI), which is a group of directors on intelligence matters, an advisory group with some members of Congress on board. But the agency that does the work is the CIA.

Star Wars City at Cheyenne Mountain ("the Cave") near Colorado Springs is the headquarters where they all meet and where all the weapons are stored above and one mile below ground. They are responsible for gathering intelligence in the first six hundred miles of space and staying ahead of possible threats to the United States. The Guardians of the High Frontier are responsible for intelligence and protection above six hundred miles.

The chart shows that Star Wars City has an Air Force Special Academy (AFSA), which reports only to Star Wars City Headquarters. This is where they supply black helicopters and U-2 spy planes—all the advanced technology.

Defense systems for the North American Air Defense Command (NORAD) are all located at Star Wars City. The headquarters is an underground facility. Our allies are there, too—Australia, England, France and Israel. The function of NORAD is to study war with weaponry and high-ranking personnel. NORAD is the command that would make the final decision to wage war with Russia, China, Iraq, North Korea or anybody else. The key allied officials met there during Desert Storm.

The 1010 Special Security Squadron reports to Star Wars City Headquarters, the center for planning and operating all spy satellites. The 1010 Special Security is both a division and a specific location. It is responsible for recovering all crashed UFOs under Project Pounce, which is part of 1010. Pounce does not exist as a specific unit, and all the personnel involved have other jobs. They meet only at extraterrestrial craft retrievals. This is how security is kept. Someone from 1010, representing the NRO, is always at a crash site, but people from other agencies would also be present.

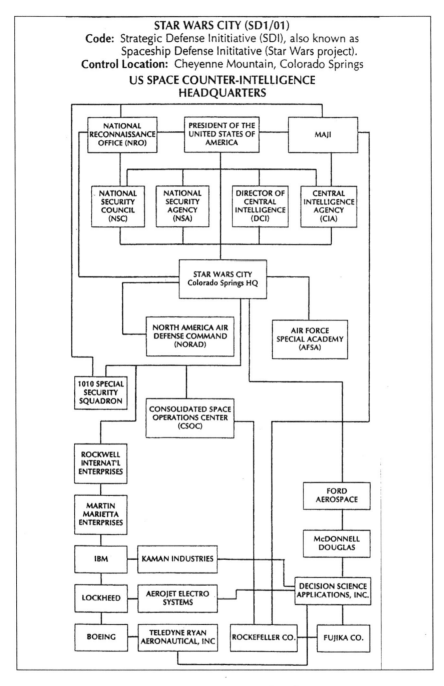

Fig. 51. Star Wars City chart.[5]

The Consolidated Space Operations Center is a group of directors from different agencies; this group issues the orders that then come out of NORAD. The Center is linked directly to the Rockefeller Corporation, which goes straight to MAJI. The chart shows that Rockefeller reports to Fujika Corporation in Japan. Rockwell International, Martin-Marietta, IBM, Lockheed and Boeing are contractors that build secret technologies. IBM, Lockheed and Boeing are directly connected to Kaman Industries, Aerojet Electro Systems and Teledyne Ryan Aeronautical, Inc., respectively. They are all involved in special projects like Lockheed Skunkworks. The chart is an indication of all the enterprises and command or operations centers that wish to see SDI continue.

Decision Science Applications, Inc., is a corporation within which our science and top scientists develop what the various aeronautical corporations then manufacture. Ford Aerospace, McDonnell Douglas and Decision Science Applications, Inc., all report to Star Wars City. In fact, all the corporations report to Star Wars City, as shown on the chart. The individual aerospace corporations do not tell each other what projects they are working on or exchange information on the projects they have been assigned; only the directors may exchange information at Operation Center meetings. It is interesting to note that Rockefeller Corporation owned Sony when Sony was a subsidiary of Fujika. The media is not shown on the chart or in the chain, but Sony, which is the media, is another enterprise that could be listed below Fujika with its own little box.

There exists a Cosmic Q, Level 33; this is MAJI, which came first. Then there is Majestic 12 (MJ-12), which is Level 32 and came later. In aircraft secret manufacturing there are directors at Level 31. Then, on Level 30, we have the officials of the Wackenhut Group and the OO-Boys, followed by the elite group of the "Snatch or Snuff," who gets orders from the Secret Service. There are thirty-eight levels to Top Secret.

I feel that the population throughout the world should know these things, and I think we should quit bypassing Congress on these issues. They should know about these matters and vote on the money so that it is not all in Black Projects, funded by black methods. You can see in the Star Wars City chart how compartmentalized and hidden this is. You can't go to any one person or place to get your answers; it is a web and that's how it works. Nobody really knows what the other guy does and no one really wants to know. In the Disclosure Project we learned how far the web gets tangled on each project.

A renegade force called the Cabal is responsible for attacking and retrieving extraterrestrial entities and craft. This may be the group that is aggressively disturbing the potential of contact between the ETs and humankind. The U.S. has already back-engineered ETVs, which are classified Ultra Cosmic Top Secret. We have an advanced antigravity propulsion system propelled by the force of an antimatter reaction. It is important to remember that the ET Network is far more advanced than we are, that even with the Star Wars program in place we would never win a war against them. I don't believe that day will come. The most important action is to now rebuild a new society based on peace.

One good beginning occurred on October 2, 2001, when Rep. Dennis Kucinich introduced the following bill, HR 2977.

107th CONGRESS
1st Session

H. R. 2977

To preserve the cooperative, peaceful uses of space for the benefit of all humankind by permanently prohibiting the basing of weapons in space by the United States, and to require the President to take action to adopt and implement a world treaty banning space-based weapons.

IN THE HOUSE OF REPRESENTATIVES
October 2, 2001

Mr. KUCINICH introduced the following bill; which was referred to the Committee on Science, and in addition to the Committees on Armed Services, and International Relations, for a period to be subsequently determined by the Speaker, in each case for consideration of such provisions as fall within the jurisdiction of the committee concerned

---

A BILL

To preserve the cooperative, peaceful uses of space for the benefit of all humankind by permanently prohibiting the basing of weapons in space by the United States, and to require the President to take action to adopt and implement a world treaty banning space-based weapons.

Be it enacted by the Senate and House of Representatives of the United States of America in Congress assembled,

SECTION 1. SHORT TITLE.
This Act may be cited as the 'Space Preservation Act of 2001'.

SEC. 2. REAFFIRMATION OF POLICY ON THE PRESERVATION OF PEACE IN SPACE.
Congress reaffirms the policy expressed in section 102(a) of the National Aeronautics and Space Act of 1958 (42 U.S.C. 2451(a)), stating that it 'is the policy of the United States that activities in space should be devoted to peaceful purposes for the benefit of all mankind.'

SEC. 3. PERMANENT BAN ON BASING OF WEAPONS IN SPACE.
The President shall--
(1) implement a permanent ban on space-based weapons of the United States and remove from space any existing space-based weapons of the United States; and
(2) immediately order the permanent termination of research and development, testing, manufacturing, production, and deployment of all space-based weapons of the United States and their components.

SEC. 4. WORLD AGREEMENT BANNING SPACE-BASED WEAPONS.
The President shall direct the United States representatives to the United Nations and other international organizations to immediately work toward negotiating, adopting, and implementing a world agreement banning space-based weapons.

SEC. 5. REPORT.
The President shall submit to Congress not later than 90 days after the date of the enactment of this Act, and every 90 days thereafter, a report on--
(1) the implementation of the permanent ban on space-based weapons required by section 3; and
(2) progress toward negotiating, adopting, and implementing the agreement described in section 4.

SEC. 6. NON SPACE-BASED WEAPONS ACTIVITIES.
Nothing in this Act may be construed as prohibiting the use of funds for--
(1) space exploration;
(2) space research and development;
(3) testing, manufacturing, or production that is not related to space-based weapons or systems; or
(4) civil, commercial, or defense activities (including communications, navigation, surveillance, reconnaissance, early warning, or remote sensing) that are not related to space-based weapons or systems.

SEC. 7. DEFINITIONS.
In this Act:
(1) The term 'space' means all space extending upward from an altitude greater than 60 kilometers above the surface of the earth and any celestial body in such space.
(2)(A) The terms 'weapon' and 'weapons system' mean a device capable of any of the following:
(i) Damaging or destroying an object (whether in outer space, in the atmosphere, or on earth) by--
(I) firing one or more projectiles to collide with that object;
(II) detonating one or more explosive devices in close proximity to that object;
(III) directing a source of energy (including molecular or atomic energy, subatomic particle beams, electromagnetic radiation, plasma, or extremely low frequency (ELF) or ultra low frequency (ULF) energy radiation) against that object; or
(IV) any other unacknowledged or as yet undeveloped means.

(ii) Inflicting death or injury on, or damaging or destroying, a person (or the biological life, bodily health, mental health, or physical and economic well-being of a person)--

(I) through the use of any of the means described in clause (i) or subparagraph (B);

(II) through the use of land-based, sea-based, or space-based systems using radiation, electromagnetic, psychotronic, sonic, laser, or other energies directed at individual persons or targeted populations for the purpose of information war, mood management, or mind control of such persons or populations; or

(III) by expelling chemical or biological agents in the vicinity of a person.

(B) Such terms include exotic weapons systems such as--

(i) electronic, psychotronic, or information weapons;

(ii) chemtrails;

(iii) high altitude ultra low frequency weapons systems;

(iv) plasma, electromagnetic, sonic, or ultrasonic weapons;

(v) laser weapons systems;

(vi) strategic, theater, tactical, or extraterrestrial weapons; and

(vii) chemical, biological, environmental, climate, or tectonic weapons.

(C) The term 'exotic weapons systems' includes weapons designed to damage space or natural ecosystems (such as the ionosphere and upper atmosphere) or climate, weather, and tectonic systems with the purpose of inducing damage or destruction upon a target population or region on earth or in space.[6]

People must understand that it is idiotic to believe that we can operate a system in space that would take out extraterrestrial life. The ETs will simply neutralize it. I want to hammer in this point, because to spend billions worrying about such a danger is insanity. It is very simple: The reason the extraterrestrials have shut down our missiles is because they *can*. And they will continue to do it as long as we force them to do so by our aggressive behavior.

TOP SECRET / MAJIC EYES ONLY

SOM 1— 01

Special Operations Manual }
No 1 - 01   }

MAJESTIC — 12 GROUP
Washington 25, D. C., 7 April 1954

EXTRATERRESTRIAL ENTITIES AND TECHNOLOGY, RECOVERY AND DISPOSAL

Fig. 52. Majestic 12 Special Operations Manual—Part 1.

MAJIC
Y

—MAJIC E
artmenta
nal securi
ACCESS to
d to perso
NCE LEV
d personne
federal la

documen
ions requ
J—12 GRO
on in any f
ribed note

TOP SECRET / MAJIC EYES ONLY

CHAPTER 1

OPERATION MAJESTIC—12

Section I. PROJECT PURPOSE AND GOALS

1. Scope

This manual has been prepared especially for Majestic—12 units. Its purpose is to present all aspects of Majestic—12 so authorized personnel will have a better understanding of the goals of the Group, be able to more expertly deal with Unidentified Flying Objects, Extraterrestrial Technology and Entities, and increase the efficiency of future operations.

2. General

MJ—12 takes the subject of UFOBs, Extraterrestrial Technology, and Extraterrestrial Biological Entities very seriously and considers the entire subject to be a matter of the very highest national security. For that reason everything relating to the subject has been assigned the very highest security classification. Three main points will be covered in this section.

a. The general aspects of MJ—12 to clear up any misconceptions that anyone may have.

b. The importance of the operations.

c. The need for absolute secrecy in all phases of operation.

3. Security Classification

All information relating to MJ—12 has been classified MAJIC EYES ONLY and carries a security level 2 points above that of Top Secret. The reason for this has to do with the consequences that may arise not only from the impact upon the public should the existence of such matters become general knowledge, but also the danger of having such advanced technology as has been recovered by the Air Force fall into the hands of unfriendly foreign powers. No information is released to the public press and the official government position is that no special group such as MJ—12 exists.

4. History of the Group

Operation Majestic—12 was established by special classified presidential order on 24 September 1947 at the recommendation of Secretary of Defense James V. Forrestal and Dr. Vannevar Bush, Chairman of the Joint Research and Development Board. Operations are carried out under a Top Secret Research and Development - Intelligence Group directly responsible only to the President of the United States. The goals of the MJ—12 Group

MJ - 12 18388 2

TOP SECRET / MAJIC EYES ONLY

REPRODUCTION IN ANY FORM IS FORBIDDEN BY FEDERAL LAW

HQ Interplanetary Phenomenon
... Technical ...
... Unit

Fig 52. Part 2.

TOP SECRET / MAJIC EYES ONLY

CHAPTER 5
EXTRATERRESTRIAL BIOLOGICAL ENTITIES

Section I. LIVING ORGANISMS

1. Scope

   a. This section deals with encounters with living Extraterrestrial Biological Entities (EBEs). Such encounters fall under the jurisdiction of MJ—12)PNAC BBS—01 and will be dealt with by this special unit only. This section details the responsibilities of persons or units making the initial contact

2. General

   Any encounter with entities known to be of extraterrestrial origin is to be considered to be a matter of national security and therefore classified TOP SECRET. Under no circumstance is the general public or the public press to learn of the existence of these entities. The official government policy is that such creatures do not exist, and that no agency of the federal government is now engaged in any study of extraterrestrials or their artifacts. Any deviation from this stated policy is absolutely forbidden.

3. Encounters

   Encounters with EBEs may be classified according to one of the following categories:

   a. *Encounters initiated by EBEs.* Possible contact may take place as a result of overtures by the entities themselves. In these instances it is anticipated that encounters will take place at military installations or other secure locations selected by mutual agreement. Such meetings would have the advantage of being limited to personnel with appropriate clearance, away from public scrutiny. Although it is not considered very probable, there also exists the possibility that EBEs may land in public places without prior notice. In this case the OPNAC Team will formulate cover stories for the press and prepare briefings for the President and the Chiefs of Staff.

   b. *Encounters as the result of downed craft.* Contact with survivors of accidents or craft downed by natural events or military action may occur with little or no warning. In these cases, it is important that the initial contact be limited to military personnel to preserve security. Civilian witnesses in the area will be detained and debriefed by MJ-12. Contact with EBEs by military personnel not having MJ-12 or OPNAC clearance is to be strictly limited to action necessary to ensure the availability of the EBEs for study by the OPNAC Team

J 12 49 MR   17

TOP SECRET

Fig. 52. Part 3.

Notes

1. A copy of this document can be obtained through the FOIA from the Library of Congress. However, it is also available on a CD, along with other documents, from Red Star Productions.
2. The Air Force dealt with the ET problem early on. The NRO grew out of the Air Force with the spy satellite program.
3. For more information, see Steven M. Greer, M.D., *Disclosure: Military and Government Witnesses Reveal the Greatest Secrets in Modern History* (Crozet, Va.: Crossing Point, Inc., 2001).
4. For more information, see William E. Burrows, "The Coldest Warriors," *Air & Space Magazine* (December 1999/January 2000).
5. "Star Wars City Chart," *Nexus Magazine*, (April/May 2000): 58.
6. *Space Preservation Act of 2001*, 107th Cong., 1st sess., H.R. 2977.

CHAPTER NINE

RUSSIAN UFO FILES FOR SALE

The KGB was the largest secret police and espionage force in history, with more than three hundred thousand agents in the post-World War II era. Many of these agents infiltrated the major Western intelligence services. The Soviet Union had countless UFO sightings, but during the Communist reign there was no public admission of a Soviet interest in extraterrestrial activity, even though files in the hands of the KGB documented UFO crashes and retrieved fragments. With the change to a free market economy, many items never before available found their way into black-market CIA hands; many KGB intelligence agents from the old regime exchanged classified UFO documents for cold cash from the CIA. In fact, the U.S. government and Russia agreed to maintain the secrecy about the extraterrestrial presence and the ETs' interest in the nuclear advancements of both countries.

Most people think that we won the Cold War. We did not. Instead, the U.S. maneuvered the Soviets into financial collapse. President Khrushchev was determined to make the Soviets the world's leader in space exploration. They rushed their programs through, even though cosmonauts died in premature experiments; they were willing to make one-way trips into space. The U.S. was more cautious than the Soviets; we watched them put up the first rocket silo and the first (publicized) human in space. We knew we could benefit from their experiences.

Fig. 53. August 4, 1968—UFO sighted at Skulte Airport in Riga,
capital of Latvia, in the Baltics.

In the beginning of the Star Wars program, Russia made the mistake of keeping ahead of the United States. They hocked everything to counter the U.S.
Space Defense Initiative (SDI)—their wheat, diamonds, oil, even their UFO
documents—to keep up with America. Mikhail Gorbachev, when leaving office,
admitted they had gone broke trying to overtake the United States. After the
collapse of the Soviet Union, Russia was informed that if they wanted credit,
they must let our businessmen into their country; otherwise we would let them
starve. The U.S. also threatened Western nations with loss of credit if they
extended credit to Russia. What could the Russians do? To maintain a rocket
silo or nuclear weapons site, one needs hard currency. When people have no
food, they certainly can't pay expensive technicians or nuclear physicists.

Russia had been collecting extraterrestrial artifacts from ET crash retrievals for
years. When I testified at the Disclosure Project, I met Vasily Alexeyev, a former
major-general in the Russian Air Force in their space communications program.
He testified that the Defense Ministry and the Academy of Sciences investigated
many sightings of UFO spacecraft over their nuclear power sites. He stated that
they would deliberately create situations to engage ET craft at a particular nuclear
facility, then direct their weapons at the spacecraft. The craft would respond by
flattening like a pancake. Here's an excerpt from his testimony:

> Reports of UFO sightings came in regularly. And evidently
> somewhere nearer the core of our leadership in the sphere of the
> Defense Ministry, the Academy of Sciences and so on, a lot of this

kind of information began to build up. And not only from ordinary laymen but from scientists and professionals as well. Military men in general are not inclined to fantasize. They only report what they see, what actually occurs. They are people you can believe. You should not forget that the arms race was still going on at this time, a struggle for military and other priorities. New discoveries in science and technology were being made all the time. The UFOs were something new and not understood. And there really was an idea that they might be some means of gathering intelligence. . . . But it is interesting that one of the official versions from the commission, including among the final points, was the possibility that UFOs belonged to an extraterrestrial civilization! That was interesting! . . .

By the nature of my work I received information from various military units across Russia, the Soviet Union as it then was. I know that that material was sent on without any explanations or annotations to the relevant bodies higher up. I was aware that there were groups engaged in investigating UFOs and perhaps something more, but at that time the level of secrecy over this question was such that all that took place was receiving information and subsequently sending it on higher up: People came to see me, but as we were military men, there were no explanations of any kind. They simply said they were interested in this or that. Then they came up with a table with pictures of all the shapes of UFOs that had ever been recorded—about fifty—ranging from ellipses and spheres through to something resembling spaceships. Witnesses were asked what it looked like, then they pinned down the locality and so on. After which all the material was passed on. As a result, it is hard to say how the work was continued, to what extent it was scientific. I knew that some kind of work was going on in the Defense Ministry, the Academy of Sciences and the intelligence services. But things were such that those who weren't directly connected with the investigations didn't know what was going on. We only provided the information. I must admit that there was an awful lot of information. And here around Moscow, above many air-defense sites, testing-ranges and other installations—those are the places where UFOs appear most often. . . .[1]

Alexeyev presented documents from Russia's foreign technology division dating from the late 1960s. His brief was titled "The Soviet Effort to Contact Extraterrestrial Life."

I spoke with him at great length about the recovery of extraterrestrial technology. We compared the advances made in the field of electromagnetic propulsion systems. In the late 1970s, Major-General Alexeyev had been in charge of a retrieval site I'd read about in intelligence documents. In one instance, when an ET craft had landed, an anti-aircraft battery began shooting at the vehicle. The command at the Soviet Airspace Radar Center had been tracking the spacecraft, but just as the shooting began, everything and everyone was paralyzed on the spot so that the craft could escape.

Germany's WWII invasion nearly destroyed Russia. At the close of the war, Russia retrieved from Germany a wide range of ET devices, documents and technology, as well as scientists and intelligence agents, similar to Project Paperclip and Operations Sunrise and Overcast of the United States. This helped jump-start their space program. The rocket systems retrieved from Peenemünde had to have costly upgrades to function properly in space. (Germany's rocket science was nowhere near as advanced as their RFC 1 through 7 or the Haunebu 1 through 5.) But by the end of the war, Russia was broke; this was the main handicap to their development of zero-gravity technology. Much could not be put into practical application, so these documents remained in their files, to be purchased years later when the Soviet Union collapsed.

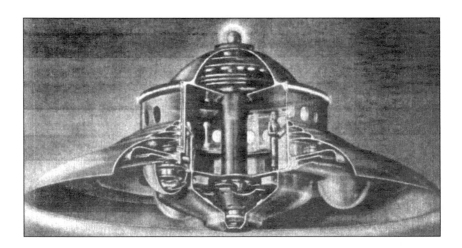

Fig. 54. Illustration of a German Haunebu.

The space programs of the 1960s were created in part to develop covert projects that reproduced ET technology. The U.S. couldn't risk losing astronauts in our space program because Congress and the public wouldn't accept such disasters. The Black Projects actually began to fund our space program after the close of WWII. A Black Project does not pass before Congress, and its funding is obtained through the sale of illegal drugs and extraterrestrial technology. This has been and still is an ultrasecret and very lucrative means of financing all Black Projects.

※   ※   ※

As mentioned earlier, our first astronauts learned that there was a civilization on the far side of the Moon. The Disclosure Project had numerous witness testimonies about our Moon explorations. One witness, Karl Wolfe, worked in the USAF and had a Top-Secret Crypto clearance with the Tactical Air Command at Langley Air Force Base, Virginia. During the early 1960s, when he worked in a division of the National Security Agency (NSA), he saw photographs taken by our lunar orbiter that showed a series of artificial structures:

> So I was asked to go over to this facility on Langley Air Force Base, where the NSA was bringing in the information from the lunar orbiter. I packed up some tools and went to the facility. A couple of officers took me into a very large hangar. As I walked in, there were people from other countries, a lot of foreign people from other countries in civilian clothes, with interpreters with them, with security badges hanging around their neck. . . .
>
> So they took me into this laboratory. I took a look at the equipment. There was an Airman Second Class in there—I was an Airman Second Class as well. He turned the equipment on and put it through its paces. It didn't do what it was supposed to do—and I saw what was going on with it. I said to him, we'll have to take this thing out of the lab if we're going to work on it. We can't work on it here in the darkroom environment. So he called someone to get some people to come in and move it. It was about the size of a small apartment refrigerator. It wasn't something you could easily move.
>
> So everyone left the facility, left the darkroom, except this Airman Second Class and myself. We're waiting for someone to come to remove this piece of equipment. So while I'm in there I said to him, "I'm really fascinated with this process, how did they get the

images from the lunar orbiter to the laboratory here?" He went through the whole process, describing how the various radio telescopes around the world were linked and they telemetered the data into Langley Field. At the time I didn't know what the real purpose of this darkroom and this operation and this facility was. I thought this was where they were bringing the data in and then releasing the images to the public. I had no idea that there were other issues involved in this facility.

So he starts telling me all of this information, and I knew that what we were doing was classified anyway and that he could only share a certain level of what he was doing with me, because of the compartmentalized nature of our jobs. At any rate, he told me how everything worked—he showed me the equipment where the digital information came in, where it was converted to photographic images. They were doing 35mm strips of film at that time, which were then assembled into 18 by 11 inch mosaics, they were called. There was a digital signature and a gray scale on every 35mm strip and those strips were from successive passes around the moon. They would take and build up a photograph. They would scan one section of the moon and then another and another and then they would get a larger image. So this mosaic then would be put in that contact printer and printed.

So he was showing me how all this worked. We walked over to one side of the lab and he said, by the way, we've discovered a base on the backside of the moon. I said, whose? What do you mean, whose? He said, yes, we've discovered a base on the backside of the moon. And at that point I became frightened and I was a little terrified, thinking to myself that if anybody walks in the room now, I know we're in jeopardy, we're in trouble, because he shouldn't be giving me this information.

I was fascinated by it, but I also knew that he was overstepping a boundary that he shouldn't. Then he pulled out one of these mosaics and showed this base on the moon, which had geometric shapes—there were towers, there were spherical buildings, there were very tall towers and things that looked somewhat like radar dishes but they were large structures.[2]

So this was known before the Apollo mission actually landed on the Moon. Astronaut Edgar Mitchell, who was aboard Apollo 14 and was the sixth man to walk on the Moon, testified that there has been deliberate disinformation on this subject. At the Disclosure Project he testified to the fact that there has been extraterrestrial contact as well as the retrieval of vehicles, bodies and material devices. He also spoke of the secrecy concerning these events for the past fifty years, which speaks to the lack of government supervision.[3]

Creating skepticism about whether we landed on the Moon in the first place by using a major TV network deflected questions about what was actually encountered there. As I stated earlier, on August 8, 2001, NBC's *Today Show* aired a segment that questioned whether or not we had in fact landed on the Moon in the 1960s. On this expedition we had placed an American flag on the Moon. This program questioned whether this lunar landing was a staged event—was the flag waving in the wind or not? (In fact, the flag was wired to make it rigid enough to be filmed clearly.)

This same kind of campaign followed the Disclosure Project's national press conference in Washington: True facts were released during the testimonies, followed by disinformation in the press. Disinformation is a mixture of "acceptable" facts and lies, meant to distract the public's attention and to create doubt and confusion and ultimately apathy.

Russia's lunar lander was destroyed by extraterrestrial vehicles, and the ETs warned the Soviets about the laws that cover inhabited planets. The U.S. was also warned, and you will notice that neither nation has returned to the Moon. Apollo 17 was our last landing, in 1972. Both the U.S. and Russia settled for an international space station. Continuing to the present, Russian and American astronauts have had visual contact with extraterrestrial spacecraft. In 1986, Russia and the U.S. were both given a directive from the extraterrestrial race occupying the dark side of the Moon: *Do not return.* In 1989, the Mutual UFO Network (MUFON) was monitoring a Discovery shuttle flight, when the voice of Dr. James Buchli came through saying, "Houston, we still have the alien spacecraft under observance."

＊　　　　　　　＊　　　　　　　＊

After the Roswell UFO crash in 1947, President Truman instituted a policy of keeping our allies, including the Soviet Union, abreast of our developing contact with extraterrestrials. The U.S. and Russia signed an agreement after Roswell to withhold knowledge from the public about the existence of UFOs and the projects to back-engineer them. The initial purpose of this policy was to inform our allies if planet Earth were at risk and to develop a response to an ET threat. (Later, an international group was formed in Geneva, Switzerland, headquarters of the economic elite. This group was the Bilderberg group, overlords of a secret program for a New World Order that would be a means of world control by convincing the population that there is an extraterrestrial threat.)

The CIA was mainly interested in Russia's advanced technologies, those using an electromagnetic propulsion system. Most of the new space technology was recovered from ET craft retrievals. Through the Ministry of Defense in Moscow, CIA agents would arrange clandestine meetings with rogue KGB agents and would often run into agents who took them for a ride. Behind the Iron Curtain deals were made, and we pretty much cleaned them out of their space technology files without public knowledge. In reverse, the Soviets paid hard currency to obtain files on American UFO craft retrievals. It all depended on what either side had to spend.

Fig. 55. Soviet nuclear missile site in the Baltics.

A few of the Russian UFO files have found their way into the public arena. Some exchanges have been secretly filmed, and most documents have probably been sold more than once on the black market of the UFO underground. A single document could sell for $10,000 to $50,000, sometimes more, depending on its importance.

The Soviets were ultimately more interested in the practical and spiritual implications of a civilization that is more advanced than any culture on this planet. They back-engineered the technology, but at the close of the Cold War their interests shifted toward a more open dialogue. Within the Russian government and their Secret Service, certain individuals began to come forward more publicly.

Fig. 56. Closeup of a UFO at a Soviet missile site in the Baltics.

Through Projects Sidekick, Galileo and Looking Glass, U.S. programs dealt with lasers, time travel, computer chips, antigravity systems, magnified light lenses and genetic engineering.

✳   ✳   ✳

On May 27, 1990, Giorgio Bongiovanni met with President Gorbachev in Moscow about ET relations with planet Earth. Bongiovanni is a stigmata phenomenon who has seen diverse aspects of extraterrestrial life. The Catholic Church wanted to sponsor him, but only under certain guidelines. They wanted him to not speak of UFOs and let the Church control his message, but he refused. He once had an experience where Mother Mary descended from a spacecraft to deliver a message. I have met with him several times, and he has told me about this experience.

He says Mother Mary represents the spirit of Mother Earth. Her pain and suffering is shown in the statues that cry tears and blood, a cry to stop the wars, the contamination of the Earth and nuclear weapons. Bongiovanni says that the extraterrestrials will stop this as their presence becomes known to the world. In February 1997, he was in a filmed meeting with a military team from the Russian government and Secret Service. The meeting was held at the

Military University of Air Defense (Tver), called the Red Flag, and was sponsored by the Russian Center for UFO Studies.

At this meeting were Professor Boris Chourinov, president of the UFO Center; Lieutenant Colonel Boris Sidorenko; Colonel Vianceslav Zhurkin of the Russian Secret Service; and Three-Star General Ghennadi Rescetnikov.[4] The Russian delegation stated that the presence and attention of the extraterrestrials were focused mainly on the U.S., Russia and the five other leading superpowers because of their nuclear weapons. The extraterrestrials are concerned—and have been for the past fifty years—with the nuclear weapons and general behavior of these nations. They are concerned about the spiritual state of these nations and their withholding information about the extraterrestrial presence on Earth.

Certain high-ranking Russian officials would like to make a public statement that would break the pact to withhold the truth, the pact made after the Cold War when the religions and military-industrial nations were determined to stay in power at any cost. The Russian representatives said that the extraterrestrials were peaceful, good and powerful and were preparing humanity for important events that will occur in the near future.

Many Russian cosmonauts had to sign documents agreeing to silence about what they saw and know about this subject. However, at this meeting Bongiovanni was given photographs by cosmonauts Vladimir Kovalyonok and Vladimir Aksyonov. These photographs were taken from the Mir orbiting station and clearly show a cylinder-shaped craft and another craft splitting into smaller ones. Furthermore, the Russians have acknowledged that the extraterrestrials have at times taken active control of military bases to implement the advanced civilization's space laws.

Bongiovanni took the film and documentation to Washington, where he was sent to NASA to handle the "UFO matter." Ultimately, a few photos were released, which can be obtained through the Freedom of Information Act. (One can obtain them more rapidly through the Library of Congress with an attorney's assistance.) Bongiovanni says that the stock market will crash and religions will be destroyed when the extraterrestrial presence is made public. Then the powers that control the world will weaken and national governments, economies, the military complex and private interests of the economic elite will collapse.

If we are to take our place in interstellar space, it will not be with nuclear weapons. Until then, Bongiovanni states, "Prayer and meditation is the conscious contact with this cosmic consciousness. But it is not enough. Action is what is needed."[5]

Notes

1. Steven M. Greer, M.D., *Disclosure: Military and Government Witnesses Reveal the Greatest Secrets in Modern History* (Crozet, Va.: Crossing Point, Inc., 2001), 346–347.
2. Ibid., 414–415.
3. Ibid., 61–64.
4. *The Truth about UFOs in Russia*, produced by Giorgio Bongiovanni, 60 min., 1997, videocassette.
5. Ibid.

CHAPTER TEN

SECRET DEEP UNDERGROUND
MILITARY BASES

A merica's deep underground military bases were begun during World War II on the mainland, in Hawaii and in the Philippines. The most noted for its elaborate system was the one in Bataan. That is when the U.S. began to build small underground cities.

When I first saw the underground bases of Bataan, I was amazed at the different complexes: whole hospitals, headquarters for the entire staff and quarters for the personnel who manned the weapons. My friend Phil Schneider learned what he knew of such construction from the archives of Bataan and Hawaii, which enabled him to foresee and prepare for the future. But we never dreamed that the future would bring such underground facilities as at Dulce, New Mexico; Wright-Patterson in Ohio; Cheyenne Mountain in Colorado; Area 51 in Nevada; and others. This is where the storage, secrecy and back-engineering of ET technology began.

Historically, whenever the U.S. found a reason to build an underground city or tunnel for whatever purpose, some part of the government or military would inevitably find a need for another. In the U.S. there has existed for many years a secret transit system for freight and passengers that far exceeds what we regard as rapid transit. Underground shuttle networks crisscross beneath every state on an endless subterranean highway system. This network and its checkpoints even cross the oceans, becoming a worldwide network called the Subglobal System. Using a Maglev vacuum, travel takes place at Mach 2, twice the speed of sound.

Because of the Roswell crash and the retrieval of ET technology, the U.S. began a new chapter in its history that involved underground construction. Phil Schneider simply knew too much about these Black budget programs that are subverting science. He paid for it with his life; he is a friend I sorely miss.

Fig. 57. Phil Schneider.

Underground Bases

A Lecture by Phil Schneider

May 1995

It is because of the horrendous structure of the federal government that I feel directly imperiled not to tell anybody about this material. How long I will be able to do this is anybody's guess. . . .

I want you to know that these United States are a beautiful place. I have gone to more than 70 countries, and I cannot remember any country that has the beauty, as well as the magnificence of its people, like these United States.

. . . I . . . went through engineering school . . . and I built up a reputation for being a geological engineer, as well as a structural engineer with both military and aerospace applications. I have helped build two main bases in the United States that have some significance as far as what is called the New World Order. The first base is the one at Dulce, New Mexico. . . .

. . . Part of what I am going to tell you is probably going to be very unbelievable; though instead of putting your glasses on, I'm going to ask you to put your "scepticals" on. But please, feel free to do your own homework. I know the Freedom of Information Act isn't much to go on, but it's the best we've got. The local law library is a good place to look for Congressional Records. So, if one continues to do their homework, then one can be standing vigilant in regard to their country.

Deep Underground Military Bases and Black Budget

. . . The first part of this talk is going to concern deep underground military bases and the Black budget. The Black budget is a secretive budget that garners 25 percent of the gross national product of the United States. The Black budget currently consumes $1.25 trillion per year. At least, this amount is used in Black programs like those concerned with deep underground military bases. Presently, there are 129 deep underground military bases in the United States.

They have been building these 129 bases day and night, unceasingly, since the early 1940s. Some of them were built even earlier than that. These bases are basically large cities underground, connected by high-speed magneto-leviton [Maglev] trains that have speeds up to Mach 2. Several books have been written about this activity. Al Bielek has my only copy of one of them. Richard Souder, a Ph.D. architect, has risked his life by talking about this. He worked with a number of government agencies on deep underground military bases. In around where you live, in Idaho, there are 11 of them.

The average depth of these bases is over a mile and they, again, are basically whole cities underground. They all are between 2.66 and 4.25 cubic miles in size. They have laser drilling machines that can drill a tunnel seven miles long in one day. The Black projects sidestep the authority of Congress, which as we know is illegal. Right now, the New World Order is depending on these bases. If I had known at the time I was working on them that the NWO was involved, I would not have done it. I was lied to rather extensively.

Development of Military Technology, Implied German Interest in Hyperspacial Technology and More

Basically, as far as technology is concerned, for every calendar year that transpires, military technology increases about 44.5 years. This is why it is easy to understand that back in 1943 they were able to create, through the use of vaccum [sic] tube technology, a ship that could literally disappear from one place and appear in another place.

My father, Otto Oscar Schneider, fought on both sides of the war. He was originally a U-boat captain and was captured and repatriated in the United States. He was involved with different kinds of concerns, such as the A-bomb, the H-bomb and the Philadelphia Experiment. He invented a high-speed camera that took pictures of the first atomic tests at Bikini Island on July 12, 1946. I have original photographs of that test, and the photos also show UFOs fleeing the bomb site at a high rate of speed. . . .

Anyway, my father laid the groundwork with theoreticians about the Philadelphia Experiment as well as other experiments. What does that have to do with me? Nothing, other than the fact that he was my father. I don't agree with what he did on the other side, but I think he had a lot of guts in coming here. He was hated in Germany. There was a $1 million reward, payable in gold, to anyone who killed him. Obviously, they didn't succeed. Anyway, back to our topic—deep underground bases.

The Firefight at Dulce Base

. . . I was involved in building an addition to the deep underground military base at Dulce, which is probably the deepest base. It goes down seven levels and is over 2.5 miles deep. At that particular time, we had drilled four distinct holes in the desert, and we were going to link them together and blow out large sections at a time. My job was to go down the holes and check the rock samples and recommend the explosive to deal with the particular rock. As I was headed down there, we found ourselves amidst a large cavern that was full of outer-space aliens, otherwise known as large Greys. I shot two of them. At that time, there were 30 people down there. About 40 more came down after this started, and all of them got killed. We had surprised a whole underground base of existing aliens. . . .

Anyway, I got shot in the chest with one of their weapons, which was a box on their body, that blew a hole in me and gave me a nasty dose of cobalt radiation. I have had cancer because of that.

I didn't get really interested in UFO technology until I started work at Area 51, north of Las Vegas. After about two years recuperating after the 1979 incident, I went back to work for Morrison and Knudson, EG&G and other companies. At Area 51, they were testing all kinds of peculiar spacecraft. . . .

Government Factions, Railroad Cars and Shackle Contracts

Now, I am very worried about the activity of the federal government. They have lied to the public, stonewalled senators, and have refused to tell the truth in regard to alien matters. . . .

. . . Our present structure of government is "technocracy," not democracy, and it is a form of feudalism. It has nothing to do with the republic of the United States. . . . I am not a very good speaker, but I'll keep shooting my mouth off until somebody puts a bullet in me. . . .

America's Black Program Contractors

. . . There are 29 prototype stealth aircraft presently. The budget from the U.S. Congress five-year plan for these is $245.6 million. You couldn't buy the spare parts for these Black programs for that amount. So we've been lied to. The Black budget is roughly $1.3 trillion every two years. A trillion is a thousand billion. A trillion dollars weighs 11 tons. The U.S. Congress never sees the books involved with this clandestine pot of gold. Contractors of stealth programs: EG&G, Westinghouse, McDonnell Douglas, Morrison-Knudson, Wackenhut Security Systems, Boeing Aerospace, Lorimar Aerospace, Aerospacial in France, Mitsubishi Industries, Ryder Trucks, Bechtel, I.G. Farben plus a host of hundreds more. Is this what we are supposed to be living up to as freedom-loving people? I don't believe so.

Star Wars and Apparent Alien Threat

Still, 68% of the military budget is directly or indirectly affected by the Black budget. Star Wars relies heavily upon stealth weaponry. By the way, none of the stealth programs would have been available if we had not taken apart crashed alien disks. None of it. Some of you might ask what the "space shuttle" is "shuttling." Large ingots of special metals that are milled in space and cannot be produced on the surface of the earth. They need the near vacuum of outer space to produce them. We are not even being told anything close to the truth. I believe our government officials have sold us down the drain—lock, stock and barrel. Up until several weeks ago, I was employed by the U.S. government with a Ryolite-38 clearance factor—one of the highest in the world. I believe the Star Wars program is there solely to act as a buffer to prevent alien attack—it has nothing to do with the "cold war," which was only a toy to garner money from all the people—for what? The whole lie was planned and executed for the last 75 years.

Stealth Aircraft Technology Used by U.S. Agencies and the United Nations

Here's another piece of information for you folks. The Drug Enforcement Administration and the ATF rely on stealth tactical weaponry for as much as 40% of their operations budget. This in 1993, and the figures have gone up considerably since. The United Nations used American stealth aircraft for over 28% of its collective worldwide operations from 1990 to 1992, according to the Center for Strategic Studies and UN Report 3092.

The Guardians of Stealth and Delta Force Origins of the Bosnia Conflict

The Guardians of Stealth: There are at least three distinct classifications of police that guard our most well-kept secrets. Number one, the Military Joint Tactical Force (MJTF), sometimes called the Delta Force or Black Berets, is a multi-national tactical force primarily used to guard the various stealth aircraft worldwide. By the way, there were 172 stealth aircraft built. Ten crashed, so there were at last count about 162. Bill Clinton signed them away about six weeks ago to the United Nations. There have been indications that the Delta Force was sent over to Bosnia during the last days of the Bush administration as a covert sniper force, and that they started taking pot shots at each side of the controversy, in order to actually start the Bosnia conflict that would be used by succeeding administrations for political purposes.

Thoughts on the Bombings in the United States

I was hired not too long ago to do a report on the World Trade Center bombing. I was hired because I know about the 90 some-odd varieties of chemical explosives. I looked at the pictures taken right after the blast. The concrete was puddled and melted. The steel and the rebar was literally extruded up to six feet longer than its original length. There is only one weapon that can do that—a small nuclear weapon. That's a construction-type nuclear device. Obviously, when they say that it was a nitrate explosive that did the damage, they're lying 100 percent, folks. The people they have in custody probably didn't do the crime. As a matter of fact, I have reason to believe that the same group held in custody did do other crimes, such as killing a Jewish rabbi in New York.

However, I want to further mention that with the last explosion, in Oklahoma City, they are saying that it was a nitrate or fertilizer bomb that did it. First, they came out and said it was a 1,000 pound fertilizer bomb. Then it was 1,500, then 2,000 pounds. Now it's 20,000. You can't put 20,000 pounds of fertilizer in a Ryder Truck. Now, I've never mixed explosives, per se. I know the chemical structure and the application of construction explosives. My reputation was based on it. I helped hollow out more than 13 deep underground military bases in the United States. I worked on the Malta project, in West Germany, in Spain and in Italy. I can tell you from experience that a nitrate explosion would have hardly shattered the windows of the federal building in Oklahoma City. It would have killed a few people and knocked part of the facing off the building, but it would have never done that kind of damage. I believe I have been lied to, and I am not taking it any longer, so I'm telling you that you've been lied to.

Some Statistics on the Black Helicopter Presence

. . . There are over 64,000 black helicopters in the United States. For every hour that goes by, there is one being built. Is this the proper use of our money? What does the federal government need 64,000 tactical helicopters for if they are not trying to enslave us? I doubt if the entire military needs 64,000 worldwide. I doubt if all the world needs that many. There are 157 F-117A stealth aircraft loaded with LIDAR and computer-enhanced imaging radar. They can see you walking from room to room when they fly over your house. They see objects in the house from the air with a variation limit of 1 inch to 30,000 miles. That's how accurate that is. Now, I worked in the federal government for a long time, and I know exactly how they handle their business. . . .

Right now, I am dying of cancer that I contracted because of my work for the federal government. I might live six months. I might not. I will tell you one thing. If I keep speaking out like I am, maybe God will give me the life to talk my head off. I will break every law that it takes to talk my head off. . . . I have spoken 19 times and have probably reached 45,000 people. . . . I cut up my security card and sent it back to the government and told them if I was threatened, and I have been, that I was going to upload 140,000 pages of documentation to the Internet about government structure and the whole plan. I have already begun that task.

Thank you very much.[1]

According to the medical examiner's report, Phil Schneider's death was ruled a suicide. However, there was no toxicology report. It was stated that there was rubber tubing tied around the neck and the death certificate states "asphyxiation by ligature strangulation." James Lujan's film *High Strange New Mexico* thoroughly investigates the controversial end of Phil Schneider's life and shows a photograph of the ligature around his neck.[2]

The information about underground bases I know is true. I believe most of what Phil said was true because he said so; he risked his life to say it. When we were in Washington, we exchanged our life stories in the UFO arena. We commented on different experiences we'd had and then began going public. The difference between us was that he didn't care if he got killed, because he had cancer. Our friendship continued with mutual exchanges that were rewarding for both of us—what I didn't know, he did, and vice versa. We became great friends until his untimely death.

What we knew in terms of Black Projects and drug money had disillusioned us both. We knew that the funding for these projects came out of Vietnam, South America and the Middle East. Our disillusionment stemmed from images of the desecration of the bodies of American GIs being stuffed with drugs in Vietnam and retrieved at Dover Air Force Base in Delaware. (By the way, there was more than that going on in Vietnam. There was a lot of ET activity, and one of the code words was "enemy helicopters." Well, all helicopters in Vietnam were ours. So when they would say in a message that enemy helicopters were in this valley or that they had taken this village, we knew it'd been extraterrestrials.) Oliver North was delivering drugs from South America to raise money for Black Projects. Again, the Illuminati is the military-industrial complex, and Phil Schneider died for his principles and what he believed was right or wrong.

If he had been alive, he would have participated in the May 2001 Disclosure Project in Washington, D.C., and we would have learned a lot more about the secrets. But they killed him because he was exposing too much. A lot of his information was on computers; he was releasing it, writing books and lecturing.

Just before he was killed, they told him that a lot of the information he was releasing was too secret to be told. He was going to tell it anyway. He told me he didn't care if they did kill him—they would be doing him a service because he was in so much pain from the radiation he'd undergone to battle cancer. His hands were crippled; he couldn't close his fingers. There were scars all over his chest. Now all his files are gone; everything was cleaned out. Phil was a patriot, like his father before him.

✳   ✳   ✳

Another major theme in covert projects and secret knowledge is that of extraterrestrials and their visits as well as recovered ET vehicles, which have been back-engineered and used by the military for secret military purposes. A break in this secrecy began recently in France. The following article from the *Boston Sunday Globe* gives this background.

The Boston Globe

| SCIENCE & SOCIETY | MAY 21, 2000 | LESLIE KEAN |

UFO theorists gain support abroad, but repression at home

Study by French officials, routine unexplained sightings, US military safety aspects combine to boost believers

Last month's release of the first detailed satellite images of Area 51, the top-secret US Air Force test site in Nevada, prompted a Web site meltdown as people from across the nation logged on in search of clues about unidentified flying objects.

"The interest has been really phenomenal," said David Mountain, marketing director for Aerial Images Inc., which posted the high-resolution photographs of Area 51 on the Internet.

But those hoping to see signs that captured UFOs are stored at the site (as some aficionados have suggested) were destined to be disappointed. Most of Area 51's operations occur underground, making photos meaningless.

Anyone looking for fresh information on UFOs would have better luck trying a new, but less publicized, source: a study by the French military, just translated into an approved English edition.

High-level officials—including retired generals from the French Institute of Higher Studies for National Defense, a government-financed strategic planning agency—recently took a giant step in openly challenging skepticism about UFOs.

In a report based on a three-year study, they concluded that "numerous manifestations observed by reliable witnesses could be the work of craft of extraterrestrial origin" and that, in fact, the best explanation is "the extraterrestrial hypothesis." Although not categorically proven, "strong presumptions exist in its favor and if it is correct, it is loaded with significant consequences."

The French group reached that conclusion after examining nearly 500 international aeronautical sightings and radar/visual cases, and previously undisclosed pilots' reports. They drew on data from official sources, government authorities, and the air forces of other countries. The findings are contained in a 90-page report titled "UFOs and Defense: What Should We Prepare For?"

"The number of sightings, which are completely unexplained despite the abundance and quality of data from them, is growing throughout the world," the team declared.

The authors note that about 5 percent of sightings on which there is solid documentation cannot be easily attributed to earthly sources, such as secret military exercises. This 5 percent seem "to be completely unknown flying machines with exceptional performances that are guided by a natural or artificial intelligence," they say. Science has developed plausible models for travel from another solar system and for technology that could be used to propel the vehicles, the report points out.

It assures readers that UFOs have demonstrated no hostile acts, "although intimidation maneuvers have been confirmed."

Given the widespread skepticism about UFOs, many will quickly dismiss the generals' "extraterrestrial hypothesis." But it is less easy to do so once the authors' credentials are considered. The study's originators are four-star General Bernard Norlain, former commander of the French Tactical Air Force and military counselor to the prime minister; General Denis Letty, an air force fighter pilot; and Andre Lebeau, former head of the National Center for Space Studies, the French equivalent of NASA.

They formed a 12-member "Committee for In-depth Studies," abbreviated as COMETA, which authored the report. Other contributors included a three-star admiral, the national chief of police, and the head of a government agency studying the subject, as well as scientists and weapons engineers.

Not only does the group stand by its findings, it is urging international action. The writers recommend that France establish "sectorial cooperation agreements with interested European and foreign countries" on the matter of UFOs. They suggest that the European Union undertake diplomatic action with the United States "exerting useful pressure to clarify this crucial issue which must fall within the scope of political and strategic alliances."

Why might the United States be interested—albeit, privately—in a subject often met with ridicule, or considered the domain of the irrational?

For one thing, declassified US government documents show that unexplained objects with extraordinary technical capabilities pose challenges to military activity around the globe. For example, US fighter jets have attempted to pursue UFOs, according to North American Aerospace Defense Command logs and Air Force documents. Iranian and Peruvian air force planes attempted to shoot down unidentified craft in 1976 and 1980. Belgium F-16s armed with missiles pursued a UFO in 1990.

Further, the French report says that there have been "visits above secret installations and missile bases" and "military aircraft shadowed" in the United States.

Edgar Mitchell, the Apollo 14 astronaut who was the sixth man to walk on the moon, is one of many supporters of international cooperation on UFOs. Of the French report, he says, "It's significant that individuals of some standing in the government, military, and intelligence community in France came forth with this."

Mitchell, who holds a doctorate from MIT in aeronautics and astronautics, is convinced "at a confidence level above 90 percent, that there is reality to all of this." He says, "People have been digging through the files and investigating for years now. The files are quite convincing. The only thing that's lacking is the official stamp."

Mitchell joins five-star Admiral Lord Hill-Norton, the former head of the British Ministry of Defense, in calling for congressional fact-finding hearings into the UFO question.

Although Congress seems disinclined to pursue the matter, the public's interest in UFOs is undiminished. A ballot initiative underway in Missouri, certified by the secretary of state in March, urges Congress to convene hearings. The initiative states that "the Federal Government's handling of the UFO issue has contributed to the public cynicism toward, and general mistrust of, government."

US Naval Reserve Commander Willard H. Miller has long been communicating this same concern to high level federal officials. With over 30 years in Navy and joint interagency operations with the Defense Department, Miller has participated in a series of previously undisclosed briefings for Pentagon brass about military policy regarding UFOs.

Like many, Miller says he worries that the military's lack of preparation for encounters with unexplained craft could provoke dangerous confrontation when, and if, such an encounter occurs; "precipitous military decisions," he warns, "may lead to unnecessary confusion, misapplication of forces, or possible catastrophic consequences."

And he says he is not alone in his concerns. "There are those in high places in the government who share a growing interest in this subject," Miller reports.

If the US military is concerned about UFOs, it is not saying so publicly. Indeed, the French report chastises the United States for what it calls an "impressive repressive arsenal" on the subject, including a policy of disinformation and military regulations prohibiting public disclosure of UFO sightings.

Air Force Regulation 200-2, "Unidentified Flying Objects Reporting," for example, prohibits the release to the public and the media of any data about "those objects which are not explainable." An even more restrictive procedure is outlined in the Joint Army Navy Air Force Publication 146, which threatens to prosecute anyone under its jurisdiction—including pilots, civilian agencies, merchant marine captains, and even some fishing vessels—for disclosing reports of sightings relevant to US security.

Although researchers have been able to obtain some information through the Freedom of Information Act, many UFO documents remain classified.

In earlier decades, issues that remain pertinent today were openly discussed. In 1960, for example, US Representative Leonard G. Wolf of Iowa entered an "urgent warning" from R.E. Hillenkoetter, a former CIA director and Navy vice admiral, into the Congressional Record that "certain dangers are linked with unidentified flying objects." Wolf cited General L.M. Chassin, NATO coordinator of Allied Air Service, warning that "If we persist in refusing to recognize the existence of the UFOs, we will end up, one fine day, by mistaking them for the guided missiles of an enemy—and the worst will be upon us."

These concerns were taken seriously enough to be incorporated into the 1971 US-Soviet "Agreement on Measures to Reduce the Outbreak of Nuclear War."

The French report may open the door for nations to be more forthcoming once again. Chile, for example, is openly addressing its own concerns about air safety and UFOs. The now retired chief of the Chilean Air Force has formed a committee with civil aviation specialists to study recent near-collisions of UFOs and civilian airliners.

As the international conversation about UFOs unfolds, sightings continue, as they have for decades. Perhaps the most notable recent US sighting took place in March 1997. Hundreds of people across Arizona reported seeing huge triangular objects, hovering silently in the night sky—a sighting that, as the state's US Senator John McCain noted recently, has "never been fully explained." As recently as Jan. 5, four policemen at different locations in St. Claire County, Illinois, witnessed a huge, brightly lighted, triangular craft flying and hovering at 1,000 feet. One officer reported witnessing extreme rapid motion by the craft that cannot be explained in conventional terms. Nearby Scott Air Force base and the Federal Aviation Administration purport to know nothing.

The Defense Department maintains it can find no information acknowledging the existence of the triangular objects. In response to a suit by curious Arizonans, it provided details of its search to US District Court Judge Stephen M. McNamee of Phoenix. On March 30, McNamee concluded that "a reasonable search was conducted" even though no information was obtained, and he dismissed the case.

There is one government agency in the country that has taken steps to prepare for a UFO encounter. The Fire Officer's Guide to Disaster Control, second edition—used by the Federal Emergency

Management Agency and taught at the seven universities offering degrees in fire science—warns of "UFO hazards," such as electrical fields that cause blackouts, force fields, and physiological effects.

"Do not stand under a UFO that is hovering at low altitudes," the book warns. "Do not touch or attempt to touch a UFO that has landed."

The text leaves little room for skepticism. John E. Mack, professor of psychiatry at Harvard University and a Pulitzer Prize-winning author, stopped being skeptical a long time ago.

"No culture from the beginning of time, no culture from anywhere on the planet, has ever voided the idea of all other intelligent life other than ourselves," he told a UFO conference at the New York Hall of Science two weeks ago. "That's arrogance."[3]

The Belgian government has also shed the secrecy surrounding UFOs by publicly acknowledging that intelligently controlled UFOs have been tracked in their airways. In the early 1990s, for the first time the Belgian Air Force publicly revealed radar images of its F-16s tracking and intercepting a UFO. This was an official publication of documents from the Belgian Ministry of Defense.

On July 11, 1991, an extraordinary press conference was held by high-ranking members of the Belgian military to brief the media about the existence of unidentified flying objects that the Belgian Air Force jets had attempted to chase down, all of which was recorded on radar screens and released to the public.

Colonel Wilfried de Brouwer was interviewed by the well-known French magazine, Paris Match, on July 5, 1990. He said that the Belgian defense system had been completely "powerless" against the tactical maneuvers of this triangular vehicle. Within a few seconds, the craft descended toward the ground to avoid radar and then rapidly accelerated upward, abruptly changing direction. It was reported that the entire episode was observed by a large number of eyewitnesses, including the gendarmes.[4]

This sighting went on for over an hour as the two F-16s, armed with missiles, chased the UFO but were unable to keep up with it. Within one minute, the craft not only was able to accelerate from two hundred to two thousand meters per second, but it simultaneously changed altitude from three thousand to seventeen hundred meters. Radar tapes of tower operators in three different towns showed the same maneuvers.

To date, thousands of people have sighted the U.S.'s Black Manta, an immense equilateral triangular spacecraft. When the Belgian F-16s were in pursuit of the Black Manta and locked on to it, the vehicle accelerated to a speed the Belgian Air Force could not comprehend. If the U.S. publicly admitted how far its technology has progressed, it would truly be an astonishing revelation. The question is, is this extraterrestrial technology or back-engineered extraterrestrial technology? The first time the Black Manta was publicly photographed was in 1988 at the North Sea when the U.S. showed our NATO allies its capabilities at a secret gathering. At that time, a citizen who was photographing lightning captured the craft on film. These craft can be parked six hundred miles out in space and left there.

Fig. 58a. Lenticular reentry vehicle.[5]

In the 1990s, there was a series of sightings of these triangular craft in the UK, in the northern territory where NATO has one deep underground military base that extends from Bentwaters to the North Sea. This is another location where the U.S. back-engineers extraterrestrial vehicles, and some of the Black Manta craft were built there.

I met Nick Pope, an official with the British Ministry of Defense, who headed the Office for Research and UFO Investigation in the UK. He testified in Washington, D.C., about the triangular craft that flew over two Air Force bases in 1993. The incident was confirmed by Admiral Lord Hill-Norton, the head of the Ministry of Defense. I was already aware of the advanced technology that had been back-engineered from a similar ET craft, which is where the technology came from. The most interesting case, however, occurred in the latter part of 1980. I heard the testimony of our own security officer, Larry Warren, who was in the United States Air Force at the time.

Warren was a security specialist who worked with the nuclear hardware secretly stored at the NATO air base in the Rendlesham Forest near Bentwaters. There was extensive documentation of the UFO crash that occurred in this area. Warren saw the humanoid beings, who were about four feet in height. They were immersed in a luminous blue light, and they were clothed. The beings did not walk on the ground but moved within the light sphere. Other craft guarded these humanoid beings. There were all sorts of light phenomena in the forest; the whole event was recorded on audiotape, and somehow Warren got the tape to CNN. Did the public hear it? No, not until very recently.

Clifford Stone later investigated the incident and spoke about the spiritual implications of such an intelligent humanoid species whose vehicle appeared near Bentwaters. It was here that a triangular object, almost like glass, crashed. It appeared to have hieroglyphics similar to the inscriptions found in the Kalahari Desert in South Africa.

Stone says it is important for people to understand that these extraterrestrial beings are living, breathing creatures as mortal as you or I. They have their loves, their likes and their dislikes. They have a culture. They are real people. We are the ones who must grow spiritually if we expect to represent humankind.

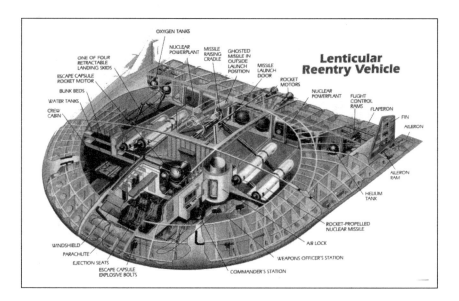

Fig. 58b. Lenticular reentry vehicle.[5]

Our government was involved in the demonstration of the Black Manta to the Belgian government. The Phoenix lights in Phoenix, Arizona, and the sightings in Gulf Breeze, Florida, were also demonstrations of the Black Manta technology. This was done to prove to our allies that we have nothing to fear from Iraq or North Korea. If they want a nuclear war, we are prepared for it with our lenticular reentry vehicle. (Lenticular refers to its shape, the strongest for weight-bearing. A round craft is easy to hide—all that is needed is to bring the temperature within two degrees of the dew point, and the ship itself can change the dew point. Then a saucer-shaped cloud appears, a lenticular cloud with a saucer-shaped vehicle inside it.)

With its pulse-beam weapons, the U.S. could destroy any nuclear weapons launched by any rogue nation. This weapons system uses multiple lasers to create hydrodynamic waves. The electromagnetic pulse technology utilized here is of ET origin. When enough particles are gathered to create mass, the resulting electroplasma light beam can do a number of things, such as push control buttons or shoot down planes. An article in the July 2001 issue of *Popular Science* featured one of these electroplasma light beams.[6]

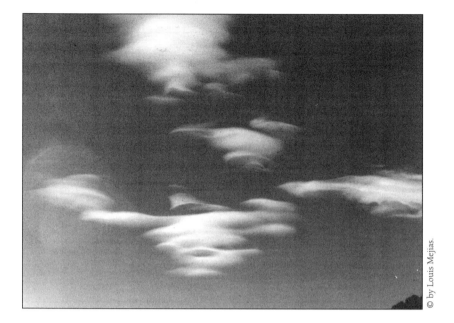

Fig. 59. Lenticular clouds, Nepal. These clouds cloak UFO craft.

＊　　　　　＊　　　　　＊

What is the extraterrestrial agenda within our own government? This mock demonstration of military technology—the Black Manta, which is actually back-engineered ET technology—is setting the stage for weaponizing space against a threat from outer space. The campaign to do this within the public arena was started and implemented by the National Reconnaissance Office (NRO) with the Development of Conscious Contact Citizenry Department (DCCCD) program. This was not spoken about in the Disclosure Project and very few people know anything about it, but that is its name and the DCCCD program is part of the NRO. They have been developing this program for a long time, and the governments of the world are waiting and watching.

Back in the late 1940s and early 1950s, there were at least sixteen crashed extraterrestrial vehicles. This is when Project Sign, Project Grudge and the disinformation program of the Blue Book began. The NSA was created not only to analyze the extraterrestrial communication and language, but to open up an ongoing contact between the U.S. and representatives of more than one network from outer space. This was Project Sigma, and the control of this information was in the hands of an international group, the Bilderbergs. As President Dwight Eisenhower took office, he was faced with these unprecedented problems, so the MJ-12 group was formed at the urging of Nelson Rockefeller, one of the leading members of the Council on Foreign Relations.

Around 1954, a race of humanoid-looking extraterrestrials made contact with our government. They were part of a hierarchy of technologically advanced species. They were (and still are) also concerned about our environment and our spiritual development; they told us to cease our building of nuclear weaponry because we were not yet spiritually advanced enough in our current state to develop weapons of mass destruction. But we didn't listen. The military wanted the ET technology, and they got it "any way they could." The Extraterrestrial Network warned us about the nuclear weapons and the technology we wanted and has appeared to governments in other countries with the same message.

As Phil Schneider stated in 1995, there were some 129 bases six years ago. By now there are more. To name a few: Pine Gap Facility, Australia; Bentwaters, England; Dulce Base, New Mexico; Hellendale, California; Area 51 (also called Groom Lake, Dreamland, Hog Farm, S-4), Nevada; China Lake, California; U.S.-Soviet Joint Base, Antarctica; 29 Palms, California; Tacoma, Washington; Ceballos, New Mexico; San Ignacio Hill, Colorado; Albuquerque, New Mexico (Manzano Mountains); Ashland, Oklahoma; Fort Stockton, Texas; Page, Arizona; Forty-Mile Canyon, Nevada; Mercury, Nevada; Deep Springs, California; Colorado Springs, Pinon Canyon, Colorado; Grand Mesa, Colorado; Los Alamos, New Mexico; Tulsa, Oklahoma; Denver, Colorado; Hudson, New York; Adirondack Mountains, New York; Atchison, Kansas; Afghanistan; northern Iran; Egypt; Alice Springs, Australia . . . the list goes on.[7]

There are projects within projects within projects—bioweaponry, genetic engineering, cloning and implant technology, intelligence-controlled medical facilities, genetic population control, mind control, remote engineering, remote technology intelligence, sonic weapons, beam weapons, plasma weapons and so on.

Information in military and intelligence groups is compartmentalized. You must have a need to know or you are not in the loop. So what do we do to eliminate this dangerous secrecy?

Even though the NSA blocked us, I recommend that the press seriously inform the American public of the recent events in Washington, D.C. [the Disclosure Project testimonies given at the National Press Club on May 9, 2001] and investigate the facts in an open, honest manner, looking for the truth rather than spreading disinformation.

I ask the public to investigate the facts for themselves through the Freedom of Information Act or the law libraries of universities. I encourage the public to tell the president to issue an executive order allowing immunity from prosecution for government, corporate and military personnel who come forward with their testimony on UFO-related subjects. I urge you to write your senators to press for open and honest congressional hearings.

It is only through public demand that the veil of secrecy can be lifted. The entire subject of UFOs should be open to a thorough study, with public involvement. The Black projects should be viewed as an identifiable misuse of our Constitution and our Bill of Rights, of "We the people" and "By the people." It is not a time to be fearful, but a time to be bold.

Notes

1. www.mt.net/~watcher/phils.html. See also *Deep Underground Military Bases*, directed by Phil Schneider, 80 min., Red Star Productions, 1995, videocassette.
2. *High Strange New Mexico*, directed by James Lujan, 112 min., Taos Productions Ltd. Co, n.d., videocassette.
3. Leslie Kean, "UFO Theorists Gain Support Abroad, but Repression at Home," *Boston Globe*, 21 May 2000, Science & Society.
4. Marie-Thérèse de Brosses, "Un Ovni Sur le Radar du F-16," *Paris Match* (July 5, 1990).
5. Jim Wilson, "America's Nuclear Flying Saucer," *Popular Mechanics* (November 2000).
6. *Popular Science*, 259, no. 1 (2001): 23.
7. From the list of underground facilities in Valdamar Valerian, *Matrix II: The Abductions and Manipulation of Humans Using Advanced Technology* (Yelm, Wash.: Leading Edge, 1991). Also see Richard Sauder, Ph.D., *Underground Bases and Tunnels: What Is the Government Trying to Hide?* (Kempton, Ill.: Adventures Unlimited Press, 1995).

CHAPTER ELEVEN

APPROACHING THE
MILLENNIUM SHIFT

According to Lord Desmond Leslie, nephew of Sir Winston Churchill, George Adamski presented a sealed document to Pope John XXIII at Vatican City, Italy. Adamski had shown Lord Desmond an extremely rare gold medal the Pope gave to him in appreciation for this secret message from extraterrestrials.

Following is an excerpt from a letter written by Lord Desmond that depicts Adamski's meeting with Pope John XXIII.

> I was in a friend's library and waiting—there was nothing to do —and suddenly I saw this book. Rather, it just seemed to jump off the shelf at me. It was entitled *Atlantis and Lemuria*, written in 1890 by Scott-Elliott and published by the Theosophists with maps of Atlantis and descriptions. It was all taken from the astral akashic records. The thing that interested me the most was their description of flying machines, which it said were circular and glowed in the dark and could move very quickly with this free energy. And they were called *vimanas*, and that got me going. I said, "Wait a minute! This is so much like the flying saucers we are hearing about."
>
> It was Captain Ruppelt who first saw them in the skies here, looking like flying saucers. So I decided that I would do a bit of research, and I went to the British Museum library, especially the Oriental section. I got a whole volume of *The Mahabharata*, a lovely

English literal translation by P. Chandra Roy—no florid, just straight literal. And each chapter, luckily, had a summary. There were about twenty volumes, and I waded through to pick up everything I could about these *vimanas*. And I just couldn't believe it—the ancients had had them, and they had been in contact with space people. And it said that by means of these wonderful craft, the star people could visit Earth and we could visit the stars. And then it described them in Tibet as like pearls in the sky.

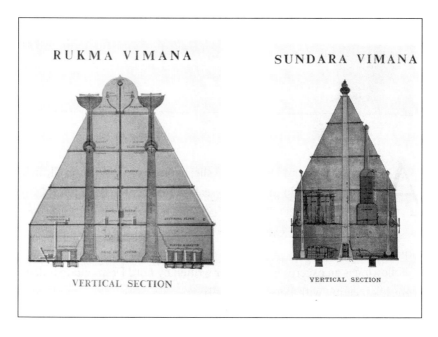

Fig. 61. *Rukma vimana* and *Sundara vimana* (*vimana* means aerial car).[3]

And then I read on, and there were things about wars in ancient India and some of the weaponry they used; they were able to make three-dimensional images of a false army—holograms surely. And there was a thing called the Brahma weapon, which had the power of the universe and the light of a thousand suns, which would tell us about the power of the atomic bomb, and it said that the survivors rushed and threw off their arms to bathe, but a few days later their hair fell out and their skin turned red and they died of a horrible sickness. And the army was so burned, even the elephants were shadows on the ground—that was Hiroshima, surely. So I said, "You know this had happened before; really, it was a space war."

Fig. 62. "Samadhi Soir" by Brien D. Coleman.

And then I got word from a correspondent in America, Sir Rick Williams, who said a friend of his had had a contact, a landing. He had taken these amazing photographs. I wrote to him and said that I had written this book about the Ancients and UFOs, and could I see his photos. Well, back they all came with a lovely letter giving me permission to use them. There was nothing about any payment at all or anything like that. They were astonishing pictures by Adamski, which were quite unlike what we thought a UFO should look like. And we had them tested for atmospheric hazing and recession and all. It came out that they were large objects quite a long way away and not little models close up.

And he sent me a rather sad little note saying that he had written an account of this landing and wanted to publish it. So the head of my then publisher, Werner Laurie, said, "If you use his photos, you are going to kill his book. So what are we going to do?" Well, we sort of looked at the ceiling and bit our nails. And he said, "Why don't we have a joint publication? Your book and then his as the second part." I thought that was a marvelous idea.

When I eventually got over to America, it was a time when you could not take any money out of England—1953. And I met this amazing man, Adamski, who lived up on Palomar Mountain with his secretary, Lucy McGinnis, and Alice Wells. They were very hospitable; making a little money hadn't affected him. And he was an incredible fellow. He would sometimes really annoy you by telling you the most absurd things which you knew weren't true. And at other times he would come out with such profound wisdom. You had to be able to filter this off. You had to sort of dig information out of him.

Now, perhaps you remember the first contact; he said he took photos and they all were burned or didn't come out because of the UFO being so near. I asked him if he had the negatives, and he dug them out and they were black. I held them up against the Sun and you could see the UFO; it was there. It really needed a lot of light for you to see it. He hadn't spotted the big oval proportions of it with perfect golden sections—a lot of little details like that.

Now I asked the two ladies, Lucy and Alice. They said yes, they had seen him talking to the space man. And they'd seen this flash as the UFO took off. And they had also, earlier, as he described, seen the big mothership. And that was chased away by a lot of American planes. It just took off and went off.

Mind you, this was in 1953, 1954, and at that time Adamski described to me how he saw these fireflies in space out of the UFO window. And in 1962 was the first Moon trip with astronaut John Glenn, who sees these fireflies in space, exactly like Adamski said. He told me that there were three asteroid belts, and I believe they found a second one somewhere beyond Neptune. Adamski said that there was another one beyond Pluto. We will wait and see.

And he told me how, when he was on the mothership, they had an amazing, amazing movie—never seen anything like it. There was no screen, and all the images, everything, happened around him. Well, that was a hologram—nobody had seen a hologram. They hadn't been invented.

Now, I told him at the time, "Surely your muses were etheric people who materialized, because Venus is very hot." And he said, "They were no goddamn spooks!" I stated no, nor was resurrected Christ. He would not listen to that; he didn't want to confuse the issue. I think that was it—he just did not want to confuse. I'm certain that some of his trips were taken astrally, which Saint Paul says is so real you can't tell the difference. Saint Paul says, "With eyes in the body or out of the body, I know not."

Adamski came to Rome, lecturing—he had been on a European lecture tour where he met the Queen of Holland, and there was a frightful row and the students tried to disrupt it. And his lectures were run by Lou Zinsstag, the niece of Carl Jung. After his Roman visit, he stayed with us a few days. I kept the press away. And we took our little boat out on the Thames and he brought out some money. And among it was what looked like a little gold coin. He just said casually, "That's a bit of gold no one is going to get off me."

I said, "Why, it's very nice." And he said, "Look at it." And it was a little medal of Pope John, who at that time was dying, John the XXIII. And he said, "I saw him in Rome and he gave me this." I said, "George, please, nobody sees the Pope; he's dying. Tell me you've bicycled around the rings of Saturn and I'll probably believe you. I don't think you saw the Pope!"

He said, "Well, I did, and he gave me this and I gave him a sealed package from the space people. He sat up in bed, and I gave him this package. And the Pope said, 'That is what I've been hoping and praying for.'" I said, "What was in the package?" He said, "I don't know. The space people gave it to me. It was sealed. I wasn't going to ask questions."

He then said, "That man isn't going to die. He looked so fit and well." Then the next day, I think it was a Sunday, the news came. The Pope was dead. And George said, "The bastards, they've murdered him!" Well, they hadn't because—and this is another interesting bit of evidence—years later the Pope's doctor told a story about Pope John's last days. How he had this form of cancer where in the last few days you have a false reprieve and you suddenly feel very young and well and you feel marvelous, and then boom! Well, that is when George saw him. We never knew that for many years.

So then I said to Lou Zinsstag, "Tell me, Lou, what really did happen? He didn't really see the Pope." She said, "All I know is we went to the Vatican, St. Peter's Square, at George's insistence. And he suddenly pointed and said, 'That's my man.' And there was a priest with red on his chest. And I commented that that was probably a priest or archbishop, somebody rather important." And she said, "They embraced like old friends, and they went off to the private entrance on the left, not the public one. And I thought, That's amazing. And then an hour later he came out, jumping up and down like a schoolboy, saying, 'Hurray! I've seen him, I gave him the message!'"

Now, the interesting thing was that he was with us for seven days before he mentioned it. If it was a load of bull, he'd probably have stated, "Look what the Pope gave me! I've seen the Pope— here's a medal!" Not at all; he kept rather quiet about it. It just sort of came out. So I thought, I'm just going to do one more test. I was at school with Basil Hume, now Cardinal Hume; we were in the same dormitory. And I asked him, "Listen, Basil, this little gold medal of Pope John XXIII, where can you buy it?" He answered, "No, not at all. You can't buy those, only the Pope can give you those!" I then told him that Adamski had gotten one, and he remarked, "Well, he must have done something very special to get one of those."

And you know, Pius the XII had a contact in the Vatican gardens. He said he met two angels and they told him there was a wonderful future ahead for our world.

But the governments of the world are so paranoid about these things because it is free energy. And it's the end of the oil and aviation [industries] as we know it, the automotive industry, for something much better, but they won't get their greedy little hands on it. So they will go to any lengths. When the oil runs out, they will probably pretend that they have discovered it and we will use it.

A UFO like Adamski's landed up in the Lake District, near Cumberland, Lancashire; two boys photographed it, Steven Derbyshire and his cousin. And we compared them, through photographic projection, to Adamski's, and they fit perfectly. So Prince

Philip actually wanted to see them, and I arranged it through the Queen's secretary, Sir Browning, who was a very nice man and the husband of Daphne du Maurier, who wrote *Rebecca*. Sir Browning was a great war hero. So they were taken to Prince Philip, but the deal was no press, no inkling. And the press begged me; they said, "Just nod and we will give you a thousand pounds." I suppose some ass would have sold the whole deal, but in those days a deal was a deal.

At one time Adamski was going to lecture in Bath and again he was staying with us. So I took him to Paddington Station. The sequence of events is most interesting. It was a very gray, dull, dark day. The porter took his bags to a first-class carriage where another man was sitting. He had this marvelous silver-gold hair, beautiful blue suit and dark Polaroids—why wear dark Polaroids on such a dark day? Apparently they don't like our light. And he radiated, he just had such an aura that I was almost knocked over. And he then took off his glasses, smiled at us as if to say, "Hello, I brought you here!"

I hadn't felt very well, and I took George out in the corridor and asked, "What do you think about that chap?" He said, "I don't know." I remarked that I thought he could be . . . I mean there was something very odd about him. This orange skin, the dark glasses. Then the whistle blew, the train took off. And I wished that I had stayed aboard because they got talking and he revealed himself with a secret handshake. He told Adamski that he was a scientist in England, pretending to be one.

The last thing Adamski showed me was his navel—he didn't have one; he had a starburst incised in his belly the depth of my finger, cut into the flesh—deep, deep, deep channels. I said, "How the hell did you get that?" He said, "I don't know. I was born with it." I said, "Who are you, George?" He replied, "I don't know. I cannot remember anything before I was four years old. My parents told me that one day a man appeared and took me away. When I returned, I was a different child."

Lord Desmond Leslie
WWII Fighter Pilot
London, England [early 1950s][4]

The Pope and the Queen of Holland were but a few of the high-ranking officials Adamski visited with concerning the extraterrestrial presence on Earth. He visited the United Nations several times and was invited to speak by the secretary-general in the 1960s. He talked to a number of people at the United Nations on that subject. He also visited President Kennedy on several occasions and even delivered a message to him a year before the Cuban missile crisis. Surprisingly, he was able to enter any department of the government in Washington; he had an Ordinance Pass that gave him the right of free passage.

Adamski was very adept at keeping secrets; he could keep the confidences of both sides. If the government told him to keep something quiet, he did not speak about it, and if the space people told him not to speak about something, he did not. He once said that his heart was a graveyard.

I believe that Adamski was a very special man; powers the world over knew he was telling the truth about UFOs and extraterrestrials. He said that the space beings have members here on Earth who live and work within our society. They have been coming here for thousands of years to walk amongst us with their message. They are concerned with our development and what we are doing on our planet, the destructive nature we exhibit. Our misuse of energy systems affects other dimensions, they have declared. Adamski said they brought messages of peace and understanding and spoke about the purpose of life. This is far removed from mind control and aggression.

Adamski died on April 23, 1965, and was buried in Arlington Cemetery in Washington, twenty feet from the grave of President John F. Kennedy. When I visited Adamski's gravesite, I wondered why this man, who was not an American citizen nor a famous soldier or hero of this country, was buried in such an honored place—our most notable national military cemetery. This man must have made a profound impression on someone in our government!

"*For in the final analysis, our most basic common link is that we all inhabit this one small planet. We all breathe the same air, we all cherish our children's future. And we are all mortal.*"[5]

—President John F. Kennedy

ROBERT F. KENNEDY
NEW YORK

United States Senate

WASHINGTON, D.C.

May 9, 1968

Mr. Gray Barker
Publisher, Saucer News
Box 2228
Clarksburg, West Virginia 26301

Dear Readers:

As you may know, I am a card carrying member of the Amalgamated Flying Saucers Association. Therefore, like many other people in our country I am interested in the phenomenon of flying saucers.

It is a fascinating subject that has initiated both scientific fiction fantasies and serious scientific research.

I watch with great interest all reports of unidentified flying objects, and I hope that some day we will know more about this intriguing subject.

Dr. Harlow Shapley, the prominent astronomer, has stated that there is a probability that there is other life in the universe.

I favor more research regarding this matter, and I hope that once and for all we can determine the true facts about flying saucers. Your magazine can stimulate much of the investigation and inquiry into this phenomenon through the publication of news and discussion material. This can be of great help in paving the way to a knowledge of one of the fascinating subjects of our contemporary world.

Sincerely,

Robert F. Kennedy

Fig. 63. A letter from Robert F. Kennedy.[6]

I did my own research on Adamski and found that he was a truly remarkable man, an unknown hero of his time who delivered to the Pope and the heads of nations instructions from the extraterrestrials. Although the Vatican does not publicly acknowledge UFOs as a reality, why do they have a telescope on the Apache's sacred mountain in southern Arizona? Perhaps to view the UFO activity and make the first announcement of their mass arrival.

※　　　　　　　※　　　　　　　※

Throughout the history of humankind and its holy scriptures, there have been reports of celestial visitors who came to Earth from the depths of the universe to teach through their prophets and messengers. According to the Holy Bible, Abraham entertained three angels. When they visited the city of Sodom, they were believed to be Earth men. When the Israelites left Egypt, they reported an angel who, like a pillar of fire, guided them toward the promised land. As Saint Paul reminded the Hebrews, "Some have entertained angels unawares" (Hebrews 13:2).

Are we a humanoid race from a universal gene pool? Ancient Sumerian clay tablets contain stories that are the earliest known source of the biblical story of Genesis. Based on Sumerian records from some six thousand years ago, science and religion converged in a cosmic connection that may have jump-started evolution.

Records indicate that humans were involved in a space race that propelled cultures outward to a nearby star system a millennium or more before the appearance of Christ. In fact, throughout the world we are confronted over and over again with tales of space-traveling gods who visited our planet to prepare humankind for a new age of knowledge and wisdom that would come as a result of the next evolutionary step.

Modern secret societies have known of these traditions and have always sought to accomplish ways to communicate with the ancient astronauts—like those who first arrived in Babylon all those centuries ago. This same secret network extends not only nationally and globally, but to other races and species as well, making us members of a confederation within our own galaxy.

Let's say that three or four thousand years ago somebody else came here and discovered this little planet and our solar system. This was a beginning.

Well, we have always had beings coming here from other places—the Orionites, Zeta Reticulans, Sirians, Pleiadians and other races. You hear a lot about the Pleiadians having come here for thousands of years.

History shows that in the past, the indigenous tribes thought the Europeans looked like gods as they sailed up the Hudson River in the *Half Moon*. Well, today we are taking a step forward—or you could say a step backward, because this also happened many, many thousands of years ago. We have to ask how we are going to adjust to the expected arrival of extraterrestrials. Will it be by osmosis? Will someday 40 percent of the people wake up and say, "I know this. I have that heritage within my DNA, within my genes," and suddenly everybody will realize the truth?

We on Earth are not so unique in the universe. The universe is populated by beings like ourselves, people at various stages of evolutionary development. There are billions and billions of planets around billions and billions of other sun systems. There are also billions and billions of galaxies we don't even know of yet. The universe is constantly expanding as our measuring instruments continue to improve, and it is itself expanding, according to theory.

We can believe there are people like us on other planets. If we think that a place such as Venus would be inhabitable, then what about other higher-dimensional, nonphysical realities we can call hierarchies of vibrations of light, levels unfamiliar to us? These vibrations allow physical tangibility. It could be like the vibrations observed in the light spectrum—ultraviolet at one end and infrared at the other, with other color frequencies in between.

The same spectrum of physical tangibility is found in the atom itself. This is true for the entire universe. We are familiar with the various physical tangibilities we know on Earth. However, there are invisible realities where extraterrestrial contact may be made. Many Earth cultures have been based on religions that contain reports of angels and invisible realities.

The knowledge of the universe is multidimensional, more than we can comprehend at present. We call this the harmonics of light, the spectrums of many realities in the science of light technology through which the extraterrestrials move. We are now approaching the merging of these worlds with our own reality.

Notes

1. See *Dan Salter UFO File I*, produced by Daniel M. Salter, 120 min., 1995, videocassette, Red Star Productions.
2. See http://home.nordnet.fr/~phuleux/index.shtml.
3. Stewart, Tabori & Chang (Publ.), *1999 UFO Calendar*, New York.
4. Transcribed from *Dan Salter UFO File III*, produced by Daniel M. Salter, 120 min., 1995, videocassette, Red Star Productions.
5. http://www.jfklibrary.org/jfkquote.htm.
6. Steven M. Greer, M.D., *Extraterrestrial Contact: The Evidence and Implications* (Crozet, Va: Crossing Point, Inc., 1999), 469.

CHAPTER TWELVE

THE WINGMAKERS AND THE ANCIENT ARROW SITE

S ome years ago, when looking for lost cattle on Indian land, a couple of cowboys found an archaeological site and reported it to their boss. He in turn contacted an archaeological society, and that is how the federal government ultimately learned of this site. Over the next twenty-two years, the site endured a couple of landslides, revealing an underground shaft and chambers. The Advanced Contact Intelligence Organization (ACIO) was originally set up by the National Security Agency (NSA) in 1950 to back-engineer extraterrestrial technology. A secret group within the NSA took over the archaeological site to investigate the strange underground chambers found there. They named this site the Ancient Arrow.

New Mexico law and Indian land restrictions barred entry for quite some time. The governor made the area a wildlife sanctuary and ticketed trespassers. The federal government then tried to take it over, because it had become a wildlife refuge according to the State of New Mexico. Because New Mexico was in a financial crisis, in order to get the funding to keep the refuge open, the governor made a deal with the feds. With the cooperation of the State of New Mexico, intelligence agency involvement began. My knowledge was gleaned from undisclosed sources at NASA when I was there investigating other UFO incidents.

Fig. 64. Petroglyph from northern New Mexico showing a nonterrestrial being.

The Ancient Arrow site is about eighty miles west of Chaco Canyon. To a limited extent, government archaeologists had gotten in after its initial discovery, but after the landslides, research members of the ACIO were notified that a shaft had been uncovered. After careful excavations, they accessed a time capsule and ultimately discovered twenty-three chambers. They successfully decoded the first of twenty-three segments of an optical disk that was found in the twenty-third chamber.

The optical disk they found contained twenty-three segments in the form of petroglyphs and hieroglyphic symbols. According to the ACIO, the artifacts embedded in this optical disk represent well over 8,000 pages of text, which indicate the future of the human race some 750 years from now.

The Director of Special Projects for the ACIO sent a classified document to all Labyrinth Group members, a group that was formed in 1963 by a scientist only called "Fifteen" [see Fig. 65]. The document indicates that the WingMakers, an advanced civilization, had strategically placed seven time capsules on the planet. One of these is at the Ancient Arrow site in New Mexico.

HQ Interplanetary Phenomenon
Scientific and Technical
Counterintelligence Unit
WA 25, D.C.

Return to ACIO

A C I O

MEMOS

[Language
Analysis]

WingMakers: Ancient Arrow Project

From the Desk of Jeremy Sauthers, Ph.D.
Director of Special Projects, ACIO

[Artifacts
Overview]

Classified Document No. 040297-14X-P17AA-23

HQ Interplanetary Phenomenon
Scientific and Technical
Counterintelligence Unit
WA 25, D.C.

To all Labyrinth Group Members – FYEO

PROJECT OVERVIEW

Based on all available research of the Ancient Arrow time capsule,
WingMakers seem to represent themselves as a future aspect of the human
race from a time approximately 750 years in our future. They represent a
version of humanity that has comprehension of the universal systems that
govern existence, or at least the laws of time and space. This understanding
permits the WingMakers to travel back in time and interact with humankind
at various points in its evolutionary pathway.

I would speculate that WingMakers have—throughout history—been
variously referred to as angels, gods, spirit guides, and, in some instances,
extra-terrestrials. They imply that they are adept at subtly interacting with
humankind in order to evolve its understanding of the cosmological
environment in which life evolves and transforms.

After successfully decoding the first of 23 segments of the optical disc left in
the 23rd chamber, I will share a small excerpt of their introduction as it
were:

"You may refer to us as WingMakers. We are most often confused with
angels, though we are actually quite human--just a future, perhaps more
advanced, version. Humans, conditioned as they are, seem unable or
unwilling to comprehend the vast diversity of living beings amongst the
cosmological planes of existence, and so, somewhat as a defense mechanism,
lump together what are distinctly unique beings. The angelic kingdom is a
different species of life when compared to the human or the WingMakers'
format of existence. WingMakers exist outside of time's focus, while their
human, extraterrestrial, and angelic counterparts exist within, and, to various
degrees, are bound by the principles of time. Our uniqueness stems from our
ability to operate independently of time while remaining human with all the
physical and mental characteristics therein."

Fig. 65. Classified memo regarding the WingMakers.[1]

The WingMakers are beings of advanced consciousness, culture carriers
who comprehend the universal systems that govern existence, the laws of
time and space. This understanding permits them to travel in time and inter-

act with humankind at various points in its evolutionary pathway. The other six capsules will be discovered as our consciousness rises and the time is right.

This time capsule was buried in the eighth century and conveys why the WingMakers came and what they did. It was meant to be found in the twentieth century; the others are also meant to be found during this century. The next one, I think, will be found in Egypt; we are learning now that Egypt, the Sphinx and the pyramids of the Giza Plateau are about ten to twenty thousand years older than we had thought. They will be proven to be even older than that. Edgar Cayce said that we would find a hall of records under the paw of the Sphinx—and two chambers have now been found there.

The classified memo included here contains an excerpt from the WingMakers' introduction found in the first segment of the optical disk in the twenty-third chamber. It reads as follows:

> "You may refer to us as WingMakers. We are most often confused with angels, though we are actually quite human—just a future, perhaps more advanced, version. Humans, conditioned as they are, seem unable or unwilling to comprehend the vast diversity of living beings amongst the cosmological planes of existence, and so, somewhat as a defense mechanism, lump together what are distinctly unique beings. The angelic kingdom is a different species of life when compared to the human or the WingMakers' format of existence. WingMakers exist outside of time's focus, while their human, extraterrestrial, and angelic counterparts exist within, and, to various degrees, are bound by the principles of time. Our uniqueness stems from our ability to operate independently of time while remaining human with all the physical and mental characteristics therein."[2]

It was, according to the WingMakers, they who were responsible for the evolution of humankind as well as biological evolution; they are the geneticists. The time capsules have been strategically placed and are from the future time; they will enable humans to understand their cosmic destiny and to become a member of interstellar space.

The ACIO, under the guidance of Fifteen, is one of the most secret agencies in the world. The governments of all the industrial nations pay for this organization. They have input and access to the knowledge this organization gains. In the U.S., the NSA is in charge of how much information is going to be released to the public. But if the governments do not release this information to their citizens, the extraterrestrials will. The information is meant for humanity, but these secret organizations have kept the knowledge for themselves.

It is my belief that the ancient WingMakers interacted with the indigenous peoples in North America and still do today. In fact, Native Americans say so themselves. We see this in all their creation stories, cultural beliefs and traditions, particularly in the Southwest. (The Anasazi, by the way, mysteriously disappeared in the eighth century. Where did they go? Researchers cannot answer that question.)

Within the encoded texts—as we shall call them—of this site, written in Sumerian, we learn how many times the WingMakers have been here, what their purpose was. They are culture bearers whose purpose is to bring the seeds of knowledge. They brought their math, which is the origin of our math, and they brought their music, leaving it as our

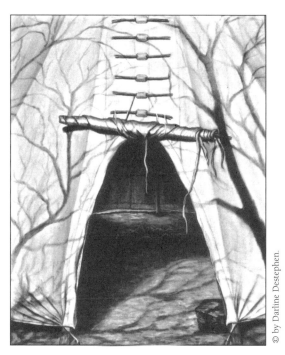

Fig. 66. "Ceremony" by Darline Destephen.

heritage. Within the chambers at Ancient Arrow are the reasons for their coming: music, math, philosophy, science, art and language. It is interesting that these texts were written in Sumerian. The Sumerians are the first people for whom we have a recorded history, and Zecharia Sitchin has written a number of books about this culture, which I recommend.[3]

※　　　　　　　　※　　　　　　　　※

You might have heard of remote viewing in terms of business espionage—selling information. Army intelligence trained people to do this. They could travel forward and backward in time and go into the secret headquarters of anybody, anywhere. It is like anchoring a double track, like remembering your dreams. You go somewhere and come back, and you can train yourself to retain that memory. Our remote-viewing intelligence program was based out of Langley Headquarters. The Russians used natural psychics early on but were concerned that the psychics were too unstable and were not strictly scientific, that the information would be unreliable. Our remote-viewing project was allegedly scrapped when we had problems with Russia. The Army announced they had disbanded the project, but it continues today.

The members of the Labyrinth Group are paid for their brains and security clearances. Most of them get easily $100,000 a year, some even more. If they rise to Level 12, they'll get more than that. "Fifteen" is a former child genius who heads the Labyrinth Group. He's probably about sixty-five now; he has been there a long time. At an early age, he went to work for Bell Labs, and within a few months he'd outstripped everything they knew. The NSA got him to work for the ACIO, and then he formed the Labyrinth Group in 1993, he took control of the whole operation, so now he really works for himself. When I was visiting NASA in the 1980s, I was at the Space Center and he was there. He doesn't look like a scientist; he had a beard and long hair and sandals. He slept at strange times, but when he woke up he'd go into high gear, like the time he assisted NASA in bringing Apollo 13 back to Earth. Fifteen was always in charge, but they wouldn't let the newspapers photograph him.

Fifteen could go into the WingMakers' chambers and telepathically read the paintings. He did not have to interpret anything, because the WingMakers would talk to him. He had been chosen by them to speak of the meanings of the Ancient Arrow site. There is some controversy surrounding his inability to get along with the NSA and the NASA. He is into what we call "Blank Slate Technology" (BST), which he calls the Freedom Key. If you have that, nobody can do anything to you.

Humanity is supposed to have this Blank Slate Technology before the years 2011 to 2018. That is why they are giving Fifteen the freedom to explore BST and the codes in the Ancient Arrow site. He, along with the Labyrinth Group, is well on his way to developing this technology. What is this BST? It is a technology that enables us to go forward in time to alter the future, to change what supposedly will have happened. You can also go back in time. Time travel is the Freedom Key. We could go back in time and erase yesterday, and whoever is in charge today would not be here. If they develop it—which Fifteen is working on—we can alter the future.

A group of extraterrestrials, far superior to most, are part of the Labyrinth Group. Somehow or other they chose Fifteen to be in charge because his mind is in agreement with both theirs and the Labyrinth Group's. The ETs have altered the future in many parts of the universe, and through Fifteen they are showing us how. He can grasp it.

Humans are moving now from the third dimension, where there are five senses, to the fourth and the fifth dimensions, where there are eight senses. We are developing those other three senses now, and some people already have them. For instance, if you are traveling from point A to point B, you know that you have left A and are on the road. The next thought you have is that you're at point B. That happens to people; it's called missing time. When you move from the third dimension to the fourth or the fifth, you jump in and out of time, you become conscious. You are there yet somewhere else at the same time. If you are in the fourth and fifth dimensions, it doesn't matter if someone has gone forward or backward in time to alter events. It wouldn't matter who has the BST, because in these dimensions you are beyond time.

We hope we can develop this technology to move beyond the time parameter, to not be affected by anyone else's plans for us. The past and the future have already happened. Therefore, you can choose where you want to view it, if you like. You can go back to A.D. 1750 and look because you have been through it already; time is not linear but horizontal and also vertical, so if you go far enough one way, you can merge into the other, like a circle.

So in a sense, if you have once been to the tenth dimension and are in the third dimension today, you came back for the purpose of helping humanity, which takes a lot of forms, not just forms like you and me. We can travel the dimensions, we can visit civilizations; all of us have already done this up to the tenth dimension. Another dimension has been formed, the eleventh dimension, and Sitchin says there are thirteen. The point is, it is endless. It never stops. In the fourth and fifth dimensions, you can think something into existence. It is like being pure energy or a pure wavelength that particlizes physicality; we can become pure energy. In order to affect the future, we need to have moved through all the levels; that is what Fifteen is working on. Although we can travel through time now, we can't step off and do anything. When we have BST, we can change the past or the future. Everybody can travel in time.

Now, there are only about three hundred people who have inside knowledge of the Ancient Arrow site, Fifteen and BST. Every now and then, an American president catches a glimpse, but this is generally not shared; it is beyond some presidential minds.

Following is an excerpt from the memo written by Jeremy Sauthers, ACIO Director of Special Projects, to all Labyrinth Group members. His memo includes translated sections from the optical disk that offer more insight into the WingMakers' mission:

> Culture-building is the primary focus of the WingMakers because it is understood to have such a significant bearing on the world of spirit and cosmological transformation. Culture-building, by definition, integrates the values of individualism with the value of oneness. It is the goal of life, as it is related to a species, to evolve itself where it can be conscious of its diverse perceptions and expressions, and integrate them into a cohesive, all-inclusive culture. . . .
>
> The underlying purpose of existence is to expand and diversify life forms in order to enable Prime Creator its fullest expression and perception of life. The human species is but one of a countless number of sentient life forms that unerringly grow and expand in diversity throughout the cosmos. It is but an atom in the Body of the Collective God. Within its consciousness, humankind is limited by its perception of the universe of wholeness by its over-reliance on the five senses. These senses are powerful forces that focus the human instrument on a separate reality much like a diver's mask can focus the diver on the underwater world.
>
> The time capsules we have left behind provide technology, art, and philosophy, indeed, an entire language that will, in time, develop two additional senses of the human instrument. The genetic composition of the human species was conceived to have 7 senses. You have, in recent times, begun to refer to the 6th sense

or the sense of intuition. There is a 7th and most powerful sense, and it is the sense that is linked to time-travel, which is linked to space travel.[4]

We should listen to the WingMakers and cultivate passion. We need to look to our future, carrying their message for all of humankind. We can make an evolutionary step into a new world, not with weapons of mass destruction, but with grace and beauty. This is our choice.

Notes

1. Jeremy Sauthers, ACIO, Director of Special Projects, "WingMakers: Ancient Arrow Project" (Classified Document No. 040297-14X-P17AA-23 to all Labyrinth Group members, FYEO). See www.wingmakers.com/arrow/acio/Sauthers.html.
2. Ibid.
3. See the books by Zecharia Sitchin listed in the bibliography located at the end of this volume.
4. Sauters, www.wingmakers.com/arrow/acio/Sauthers.html.

BIBLIOGRAPHY

Books

Baigent, Michael, Richard Leigh and Henry Lincoln. *Holy Blood, Holy Grail*. New York: Dell, 1983.

Bamford, James. *Body of Secrets: Anatomy of the Ultra-Secret National Security Agency*. New York: Anchor Books, 2002.

———. *The Puzzle Palace: A Report on America's Most Secret Agency*. New York: Viking Press, 1983.

Begich, Nick and Jeane Manning. *Angels Don't Play That HAARP*. Anchorage: Earthpulse Press, 1997.

Blavatsky, Helena Petrovna. *Isis Unveiled*. Pasadena, Calif.: Theosophical University Press, 1999.

Borklund, C.W. *The Department of Defense*. New York: HarperCollins, 1985.

Branton. *The Dulce Wars: Underground Alien Bases and the Battle for Planet Earth*. London: Inner Light Publications, 1999.

Brother Philip [George Hunt Williamson]. *Secret of the Andes*. Bolinas, Calif.: Leaves of Grass Press, 1976.

Brugger, Karl. *The Chronicle of Akakor.* New York: Delacorte Press, 1977.

Cervé, Wishar S. *Lemuria: The Lost Continent of the Pacific.* Vol. XII. San Jose: Rosicrucian Press, 1931.

Chatelain, Maurice. *Our Ancestors Came from Space.* New York: Dell, 1978.

Cooper, William. *Behold a Pale Horse.* Flagstaff, Ariz.: Light Technology Publishing, 1991.

Cotterell, Maurice. *Supergods: The Mayan Prophecies.* London: HarperCollins, 1996.

Godwin, Joscelyn, trans. *The Chemical Wedding of Christian Rosenkreutz.* Kimball, Mich.: Phanes Press, 1991.

Goetz, Delia and Sylvanus G. Morley. *Popol Vuh: The Sacred Book of the Ancient Quiché Maya.* English version from the translation of Adrián Recinos. Norman: University of Oklahoma Press, 1950.

Greer, Steven M. *Disclosure: Military and Government Witnesses Reveal the Greatest Secrets in Modern History.* Crozet, Va.: Crossing Point, Inc., 2001.

———. *Extraterrestrial Contact: The Evidence and Implications.* Crozet, Va.: Crossing Point, Inc., 1999.

Hall, Manly P. *Lost Keys of Freemasonry.* Los Angeles: Philosophical Research Society, 1976.

———. *The Secret Teachings of All Ages: An Encyclopedic Outline of Masonic, Hermetic, Qabbalistic and Rosicrucian Symbolical Philosophy.* Los Angeles: Philosophical Research Society, 1928.

Hawking, Stephen W. *A Brief History of Time: From the Big Bang to Black Holes.* New York: Bantam Books, 1988.

Henry, William. *One Foot in Atlantis.* Anchorage: Earthpulse Press, 1998.

Higham, Charles. *Trading with the Enemy: An Exposé of the Nazi-American Money Plot.* New York: Delacorte, 1983.

Icke, David. *Alice in Wonderland and the World Trade Center Disaster: Why the Official Story of 9/11 Is a Monumental Lie*. Ryde, Isle of Wight: Bridge of Love Publications, 2002.

———. *. . . And the Truth Shall Set You Free: The Most Explosive Book of the 20th Century*. Ryde, Isle of Wight: Bridge of Love Publications, 1998.

———. *The Biggest Secret: The Book That Will Change the World*. 2nd ed. Ryde, Isle of Wight: Bridge of Love Publications, 1999.

———. *Children of the Matrix: How an Interdimensional Race Has Controlled the World for Thousands of Years—And Still Does*. Ryde, Isle of Wight: Bridge of Love Publications, 2001.

———. *Robot's Rebellion: The Story of the Spiritual Renaissance*. Bath, England: Gateway Books, 1994.

Isaacson, Walter and Evan Thomas. *The Wise Men: Six Friends and the World They Made*. New York: Simon and Schuster, 1986.

Kissinger, Henry. *Nuclear Weapons and Foreign Policy*. New York: Harper & Brothers, 1957.

Klarer, Elizabeth. *Beyond the Light Barrier*. Aylesbury, UK: Howard Timmins Publishers, 1980.

Knight, Christopher and Robert Lomas. *The Hiram Key: Pharaohs, Freemasons and the Secret Discovery of the Secret Scrolls of Jesus*. Flint, Mich.: Arrow Paperback, 1997.

Kwitney, Jonathan. *The Crimes of Patriots: A True Tale of Dope, Dirty Money and the CIA*. New York: W.W. Norton, 1987.

Ledeen, Michael A. *Perilous Statecraft*. New York: Charles Scribner's Sons, 1988.

Leslie, Desmond and George Adamski. *Flying Saucers Have Landed*. New York: The British Book Centre, 1953.

Lévi, Eliphas. *The History of Magic*. Translated by Arthur Edward Waite. London: Rider & Company, 1957.

———. *Transcendental Magic*. Translated by Arthur Edward Waite. York Beach: Red Wheel/Weiser, 1968.

Lewin, Leonard. *Report from Iron Mountain on the Possibility and Desirability of Peace*. New York: Dial Press, 1962.

Maccabee, Bruce S. *The UFO-FBI Connection*. St. Paul: Llewellyn Publications, 2000.

Marrs, Jim. *Rule by Secrecy: The Hidden History That Connects the Trilateral Commission, the Freemasons, and the Great Pyramids*. New York: HarperCollins, 2000.

Melchizedek, Drunvalo. *The Ancient Secret of the Flower of Life*. 2 vols. Flagstaff, Ariz.: Light Technology Publishing, 1999.

Nichols, Preston B. with Peter Moon. *The Montauk Project: Experiments in Time*. New York: Sky Books, 1992.

Ranelagh, John. *The Agency: The Rise and Decline of the CIA*. New York: Simon & Schuster, 1986.

Redfern, Nick. *The FBI Files: The FBI's UFO Top Secrets Exposed*. London: Simon & Schuster, 1999.

Red Star, Nancy. *Legends of the Star Ancestors: Stories of Extraterrestrial Contact from Wisdomkeepers around the World*. Rochester, Vt.: Destiny Books, 2002.

———. *Star Ancestors: Indian Wisdomkeepers Share the Teachings of the Extraterrestrials*. Rochester, Vt.: Destiny Books, 2000.

Royal, Lyssa. *The Prism of Lyra*. Rev. ed. Flagstaff, Ariz.: Light Technology Publishing, 1993.

Sauder, Richard. *Underground Bases and Tunnels: What Is the Government Trying to Hide?* Kempton, Ill.: Adventures Unlimited Press, 1995.

Sitchin, Zecharia. *The Cosmic Code*. Rochester, Vt.: Bear & Company, 2002.

———. *Divine Encounters: A Guide to Visions, Angels and Other Emissaries.* Rochester, Vt.: Bear & Company, 2002.

———. *Genesis Revisited: Is Modern Science Catching Up with Ancient Knowledge?* Rochester, Vt.: Bear & Company, 1991.

———. *The Lost Book of Enki: Memoirs and Prophecies of an Extraterrestrial God.* Rochester, Vt.: Bear & Company, 2001.

———. *The Lost Realms*. Rochester, Vt.: Bear & Company, 1990.

———. *The Stairway to Heaven*. Rochester, Vt.: Bear & Company, 1993.

———. *The 12th Planet*. Rochester, Vt.: Bear & Company, 1977.

———. *The Wars of Gods and Men*. Rochester, Vt.: Bear & Company, 1992.

———. *When Time Began*. Rochester, Vt.: Bear & Company, 1994.

Steckling, Fred. *We Discovered Alien Bases on the Moon*. Vista, Calif.: GAF International, 1997.

Tansley, David V. *Chakras: Rays and Radionics*. Woodstock, N.Y.: Beekman Publishers, Inc., 1984.

Tedlock, Dennis, trans. *Popol Vuh: The Definitive Edition of the Mayan Book of the Dawn of Life and the Glories of Gods and Kings.* New York: Simon & Schuster, 1958.

Valerian, Valdamar. *Matrix I: Understanding Aspects of Covert Interaction with Alien Culture, Technology and Planetary Power Structure.* Yelm, Wash.: Leading Edge, 1988.

————. *Matrix II: The Abductions and Manipulation of Humans Using Advanced Technology.* Yelm, Wash.: Leading Edge, 1991.

————. *Matrix III: The Psychosocial, Chemical, Biological and Electromagnetic Manipulation of Human Consciousness.* Yelm, Wash.: Leading Edge. 1992.

————. *Matrix IV: The Equivideum, Paradigms and Dimensions of Human Evolution and Consciousness.* Yelm, Wash.: Leading Edge, 1994.

Webster, Nesta. *World Revolution: The Plot Against Civilization.* Sedona, Ariz.: Veritas Publishing, 1994.

Wood, David. *Genisis: The First Book of Revelations.* Kent, England: Baton Press, 1985.

Periodicals

Burrows, William E. "The Coldest Warriors." *Air & Space Magazine* (December 1999/January 2000).

De Brosses, Marie-Thérèse. "Un Ovni Sur le Radar du F-16." *Paris Match* (July 5, 1990).

"Star Wars City Chart." *Nexus Magazine,* (April/May 2000): 58.

Popular Science 256, no. 1 (2001): 23.

Wilson, Jim. "America's Nuclear Flying Saucer." *Popular Mechanics* (November 2000).

Newspaper Articles

Duin, Julia. "Government Is Covering Up UFO Evidence, Group Says." *Washington Times* 10 May 2001, Section A.

Kean, Leslie. "UFO Theorists Gain Support Abroad, but Repression at Home." *Boston Globe,* 21 May 2000, Science & Society.

Sciolino, Elaine. "Cameras Are Being Turned on a Once-Shy Spy Agency." *New York Times* 6 May 2001, Travel Section.

"Floating Mystery Ball Is New Nazi Air Weapon." *New York Times* 14 December 1944. Page 10.

Videocassettes and Films

Angels Don't Play That HAARP. Nick Begich and Jeane Manning. 105 min. Earthpulse Press, 1997. Videocassette.

Covenant of Iron Mountain. A Dan Salter film. Red Star Productions, n.d. Videocassette.

Dan Salter UFO File I. Produced by Daniel M. Salter. 120 min. Red Star Productions, 1995. Videocassette.

Dan Salter UFO File II. Produced by Daniel M. Salter. 120 min. Red Star Productions, 1995. Videocassette.

Dan Salter UFO File III. Produced by Daniel M. Salter. 120 min. Red Star Productions, 1995. Videocassette.

Deep Underground Military Bases. Directed by Phil Schneider. 80 min. Red Star Productions, 1995. Videocassette.

Fractals: The Color of Infinity. Directed by Nigel Lesmoir-Gordon. 54 min. 1994. Videocassette.

High Strange New Mexico. Directed by James Lujan. 112 min. Taos Productions Ltd. Co., n.d. Videocassette.

Holes in Heaven. Directed by Wendy Robbins. 51 min. Gallina Projects and Paula Randol-Smith Productions, 1998. Videocassette.

Koyaanisqatsi. Produced and directed by Godfrey Reggio. 87 min. Institute for Regional Education, 1982. Film.

Shadow of the Templars. Produced by Henry Lincoln. 60 min. A&E Ancient Mysteries, 1979. Videocassette.

The Thule Society. Daniel M. Salter Archives. 51 min. Red Star Productions, n.d. Videocassette.

The Truth about UFOs in Russia. Produced by Giorgio Bongiovanni. 60 min. 1997. Videocassette.

Other Sources

Cooper, William. "Operation Majority—Final Release." California: William Cooper, 1989.

Monongye, David (Hopi Elder), "Holding Fast to the Path of Peace: A Traditional View." N.p., n.d.

Pea Research. *Government Involvement in the UFO Cover-up Chronology.* California: Pea Research, 1988.

Salter, Daniel M. Archives. O.S.S., Thule Society, Victor Schauberger and Nazi archives, including German Antarctic film footage. Red Star Productions.

Sauthers, Jeremy, ACIO Director of Special Projects. "WingMakers: Ancient Arrow Project." Classified Document No. 040297-14X-P17AA-23.

Stewart, Tabori & Chang (Publ.). *1999 UFO Calendar.* New York.

Space Preservation Act of 2001, 107th Cong., 1st sess., H.R. 2977.

Web Pages

www.disclosureproject.org
http://eisenhower.archives.gov/farewell.htm
http://home.nordnet.fr/~phuleux/index.shtml
www.mt.net/~watcher/phils.html
www.nancyredstar.com
http://psychicspy.com/nsa-psy.txt
http://www.qtm.net/~geibdan/newsa/reagan.html
http://www.reagan.utexas.edu/resource/speeches/1985/120485a.htm
http://www.sacredroad.org
www.wingmakers.com/arrow/acio/Sauthers.html

SHAMANIC SECRETS for PHYSICAL MASTERY

COMING SOON

The purpose of this book is to allow you to understand the sacred nature of your own physical body and some of the magnificent gifts it offers you. When you work with your physical body in these new ways, you will discover not only its sacredness, but how it is compatible with Mother Earth, the animals, the plants, even the nearby planets, all of which you now recognize as being sacred in nature. It is important to feel the value of oneself physically before one can have any lasting physical impact on the world. The less you think of yourself physically, the less likely your physical impact on the world will be sustained by Mother Earth. If a physical energy does not feel good about itself, it will usually be resolved; other physical or spiritual energies will dissolve it because it is unnatural. The better you feel about your physical self when you do the work in the previous book as well as this one and the one to follow, the greater and more lasting will be the benevolent effect on your life, on the lives of those around you and ultimately on your planet and universe. SOFTCOVER 600P.

$**19**^{95}$ ISBN 1-891824-29-5

Chapter Titles:

- Cellular Clearing of Traumas, Unresolved Events
- Cellular Memory
- Identifying Your Body's Fear Message
- The Heart Heat Exercise
- Learn Hand Gestures
  —Remove Self-Doubt
  —Release Pain or Hate
  —Clear the Adrenals or Kidneys
  —Resolve Sexual Dysfunction
- Learning the Card Technique for Clarifying Body Message
- Seeing Life as a Gift
- Relationship of the Soul to Personality
- The New Generation of Children
- The Creator and Religions
- Food, Love & Addictions

- Communication of the Heart
- Dreams & Their Significance
- The Living Prayer/Good Life
- Life Force and Life Purpose
- Physical Mastery
- His Life/Mandate for His Ancestors/ Importance of Animals/Emissaries
- Physical Mastery
- Talking to Rain/Bear Claw Story
- Disentanglement
- Grief Culture
- Closing Comments

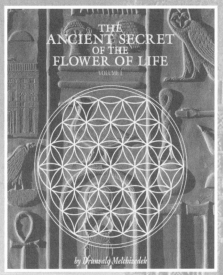

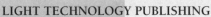

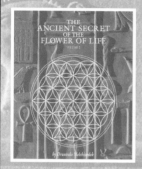

Announcing a special book
2004 PREDICTIONS
available for Oct. 2003

Note: Author photos as appeared on 2003 edition.

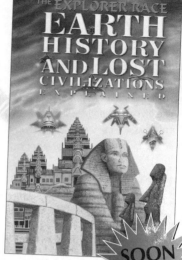